The Writing
of the Christian Gospels

The Writing of the Christian Gospels

RICK HERRICK

WIPF & STOCK · Eugene, Oregon

THE WRITING OF THE CHRISTIAN GOSPELS

Copyright © 2025 Rick Herrick. All rights reserved. Except for brief quotations in critical publications or reviews, no part of this book may be reproduced in any manner without prior written permission from the publisher. Write: Permissions, Wipf and Stock Publishers, 199 W. 8th Ave., Suite 3, Eugene, OR 97401.

Wipf & Stock
An Imprint of Wipf and Stock Publishers
199 W. 8th Ave., Suite 3
Eugene, OR 97401

www.wipfandstock.com

PAPERBACK ISBN: 979-8-3852-3789-0
HARDCOVER ISBN: 979-8-3852-3790-6
EBOOK ISBN: 979-8-3852-3791-3

VERSION NUMBER 01/15/25

Scripture quotes are from the Jerusalem Bible © 1985, Darton, Longman, and Todd, Ltd.

For Jannie, with profound gratitude and appreciation.

Contents

Acknowledgments | ix

Introduction | xi

1. Background Considerations | 1
2. The Gospel of Mark | 22
3. The Gospel of Matthew | 45
4. The Gospel of Luke | 64
5. The Gospel of John | 86
6. Conclusion | 106

Bibliography | 115

Acknowledgments

I would like to thank Ann Bassett for stimulating the creation of this book and Bob Coe for his careful reading of an earlier draft. Special thanks go to Ed Hand for his help with issues of clarity and grammar. If the arguments are clearly presented with a minimum of grammatical errors, it is because of his good work.

    I was three-and-a-half years old lying in my bed staring up at model airplanes hanging from the ceiling when my father came running up the stairs to my bedroom to announce the good news—his gospel proclamation. He had a little girl and her name was Jannie, my sister. In the seventy-five years that have followed, she has always represented good news—a warm smile, a loving welcome whenever I visit, and generous praise for my writing. Even more impressive, she lives the teachings of Jesus. It's a central focus of her life. Her example inspires me to do better. For all of the above reasons, it is my great honor to dedicate this book to her.

    Finally, I would like to thank the Wipf and Stock staff for their help with copyediting and all the many tasks involved in putting a book like this together. They are a great group of professionals to work with.

Introduction

THE IDEA FOR THIS book came as a result of unusual circumstances. The host of a local television show was interested in doing a series on the New Testament. She came to me, and we decided on the topic of the writing of the Christian Gospels. Four one-hour shows were planned.

To prepare, I made a detailed outline of the topics to be covered in the four shows. When I got back together with the TV host, she wanted to turn an interview show into a lecture series. Because that sounded rather boring to me, we scrapped the idea of a series on the writing of the Gospels and decided instead on a question-and-answer show taken from my writings and her questions. That left me with a detailed outline on the writing of the four Gospels. Because it's a fascinating story, I decided to convert the outline into a book. The first draft went quickly. The final version resulted from several years of on-again, off-again reflection and work.

A few explanatory notes are necessary before we get started. I will use traditional notations for Jewish and Christian scriptures because I find the terms "Old Testament" and "New Testament" more specific and less likely to lead to confusion. By adopting this strategy, I do not imply in any way that Christian scripture represents a higher form of revelation than Jewish scriptures. The texts from both religions were written by human beings with their own challenges, problems, and special stories of inspiration. I will, however, use CE for Common Era, which replaces AD, and BCE for before the Common Era, a replacement for BC.

Introduction

Fifty-five years ago I purchased my first Bible, *The Jerusalem Bible*, for a New Testament class I was taking in college. Our professor chose this Bible because it was written in plain English and because it came with introductions for each book and explanatory notes scattered throughout. The Gospel references cited in this book come from *The Jerusalem Bible*.

You will quickly notice biblical references follow practically every point made in the book. It is important for you to check these references especially if you come across something you don't understand or have difficulty agreeing with. Because I know most of you won't do that, I'm going to make an offer. I will pay anyone one hundred dollars if they discover a passage I have misused or misrepresented.

I make this offer because I want readers to have confidence in the passages I cite, but there are two qualifications. First, I will only pay the first person who discovers a problem. I can't afford someone ganging up on me and telling all their friends, "Hey, let's get this guy." I will send a picture of a canceled check to all those who respond too late. Second, if I can show the point I am making conforms with mainline biblical scholarship, I will write a letter listing authors that support my position which will not include a check. Please email me at rherrick86@gmail.com with questions or any problems you discover. I look forward to hearing from you.

1

Background Considerations

THE GREAT WAR

WE WILL BEGIN OUR discussion of how the Gospels were written by looking at several background factors that are crucial for understanding how the writing process unfolded. Perhaps the most significant was the Roman/Jewish War from 66 CE to 73 CE. Palestine during the time of Jesus was a Roman colony. There was widespread discontent as a result of burdensome Roman taxes and threats to Jewish culture. While the Galilee of Jesus was relatively calm during his lifetime under the rule of Herod Antipas, the situation rapidly deteriorated from 40–66 CE, which led to direct Roman rule to stem the chaos. In 66, Jewish freedom fighters seized the Roman fortress at Masada and then proceeded to throw the Romans out of Jerusalem. Rome eventually counterattacked with sixty thousand troops. In 70 CE, Roman troops entered Jerusalem, burned the entire city, and destroyed the temple. Mass crucifixions ensued with tens of thousands of Jews killed. Many others were enslaved. A few lucky ones were able to flee. Jerusalem ceased to exist as a city. It became a ghost town. The Romans did not want Jews in Jerusalem, with the result that those who survived were scattered throughout the Hellenistic world.

The Writing of the Christian Gospels

The Jesus movement was forced to move from Jerusalem to the Hellenistic world. There was a well-organized Jesus movement in Jerusalem under James, Jesus' brother, that came into existence soon after the crucifixion. These followers obviously collected and wrote down stories about Jesus. Sadly, these stories were lost. Hard historical data regarding the life and ministry of Jesus disappeared. If Gospels were written in Palestine before 70, they have never been found. Eyewitnesses were killed. The only historical data we have from first-century Palestine concerning Jesus comes from the oral tradition, which is one of the subjects discussed later in this chapter.

Because of this data problem, Jesus is described in the Gospels through story and imagination. The Gospels are by and large works of fiction. This is a scary idea for many Christians, and yet it is important to note that this was the ancient way. Most ancient biographies were based extensively on fiction. They were generally written long after the person under study had died. Hard, historical data was not available. The Gospels are not unique in this regard.

It is also important to be absolutely clear about this point. I am not going to argue the Gospel writers invented stories about Jesus because they wanted to lie or inflate his reputation. They deeply believed in the larger truth that their stories expressed. The problem was they had no solid historical data relating to the life of Jesus other than the fact that he was born a Jew, was a teacher, and was crucified. There was no information as to where Jesus was on a particular day. There was no information on a specific event he was alleged to have participated in. This kind of information was lost. A story in a Gospel may be based on historical memory, but many of the details had to be invented. There was no other alternative because reliable historical evidence did not exist.

When we moderns evaluate biographies, the most important criterion is historical accuracy. Ancients didn't have that luxury. They lacked objective historical data. For ancients, historical truth was replaced with plausibility. Is the story believable? Does it communicate meaning? Does the story tell us something important about the character of the person under study? Is the life portrayed

Background Considerations

worthy of moral emulation? These factors were what was important to ancient readers and listeners.

In light of these facts, ancient writers manipulate and create events in ways that would be unacceptable by modern standards. The New Testament Gospels are no exception. On the other hand, stories about Jesus survived a devastating war and movement into a foreign culture. The oral tradition that was passed down would not have been possible without some amazing events propelling it.

There was another important consequence of this war. Jewish eschatological expectations reached a fever pitch. Eschatology concerns ideas about the fulfillment of history when God will intervene to restore the territorial integrity of Israel, punish her enemies, rebuild the temple, and bring everlasting peace. To understand this important set of beliefs within Judaism, it is necessary to briefly review Israel's history.

When Moses led his people out of Egypt as described in the book of Exodus, he and God made a covenant on Mount Sinai. In the covenant, God promised to protect Israel in return for Jews obeying God's law. This agreement seemed to work out well for a long time. Israel flourished under Kings David and Solomon.

Things started falling apart after Solomon's death around 1000 BCE. Israel split into a northern and southern kingdom. This weakened state allowed Assyria to conqueror the Northern Kingdom in 722 BCE. Babylon captured Judah, the Southern Kingdom, two hundred years later. As a result, Israel became a colonized nation.

How could this happen? The covenant said God was supposed to protect Israel. The prophets answered this question by saying that God was no longer protecting Israel because Israel had sinned by failing to obey God's law. Israel was therefore responsible for breaking the covenant, not God. The message of the prophets was not only about punishment, however. Their collective anger over Israel's sin was always tempered by hope. That hope was the salvation of Israel as a nation. The idea was that God would honor his covenant by sending a messiah to rescue Israel. This messiah in the person of a king or a great military leader would restore Israel's glory as a nation. This messiah would establish God's kingdom on earth.

The prophetic answer worked for many years until the second century BCE. At that time a nasty Syrian king named Antiochus IV Epiphanes came into power with the goal of increasing his country's control over Israel. He set out to destroy Judaism. He ordered icons of Greek gods to be installed in the temple at Jerusalem. Pigs, an animal that is an abomination to Jews, were sacrificed on the temple altar, and he began executing Jews for circumcising their children. Jews were now being punished for obeying God's law. The answer from the prophets no longer worked.

Into this void of meaning and despair, the prophet Daniel came to the rescue. Daniel argued that Israel's misery was not the result of divine punishment, but rather the actions of Satan, the power of evil. This Satan was out to control the world. God, however, would honor his promises. There would soon come an "end times," a time that was so bad God would intervene to rescue the righteous among the people of Israel. He would do that by sending his divine agent, the Son of Man, from the clouds of heaven to judge the people of Israel and rescue the righteous by taking them to heaven. The expectation of the time when these events would take place was imminent.

These ideas pertaining to the "end times" affected Gospel writing in important ways. The horrible war and the destruction of God's city in 70 CE convinced many Jews living in the Hellenistic world where the Gospels were written that the "end times" were here. The intervention of God was imminent, within the generation of Jesus' followers. You see this sense of imminence best expressed in the Gospel of Mark, but a similar view was also held by the editors who put together Matthew and Luke. The apostle Paul had a similar view of the end times.

> The time is fulfilled, and the kingdom of God is close at hand. Repent and believe the gospel. (Mark 1:15; see also Mark 9:1)

Jesus accepted many of these ideas, which became known as Jewish apocalypticism. During his lifetime Roman colonialism was oppressing Israel. This oppression was seen as evil and representing

Background Considerations

the power of Satan. In the Synoptic Gospels of Mark, Matthew, and Luke, Jesus is seen as battling Satan through his exorcising demons and curing disease. Disease and demon possession were thought to be caused by Satan invading the body. Because Jesus was seen defeating Satan through these healing acts, he and his followers expected the kingdom of God would soon arrive. This kingdom would be on earth for the people of Israel.

Because of the total destruction of Jerusalem in 70 CE, the early church began to think differently about Jewish apocalypticism. The state of Israel had ceased to exist and therefore could no longer be redeemed. As a result, salvation was no longer pictured as a corporate concept for a nation, but for individual believers in Jesus as the Christ. These believers, the righteous, would be rescued by the Son of Man and taken to heaven. What is fascinating is that these two concepts of salvation, the idea of salvation for the nation of Israel and the contrasting idea of salvation in heaven for individual believers, float freely, alongside each other, in the Gospels. It becomes a fun challenge to figure out which concept is being trumpeted, a topic discussed in greater detail in chapter 2.

As an aside, an interesting question pertains to the book of Daniel. There is a big problem with Daniel's prophecy of rescue by the Son of Man with salvation in heaven, which provides the basis for the Christian belief in the second coming. Unfortunately, the book of Daniel does not reflect the word of God, but is rather a fraudulent work.

Here's the problem. Daniel claims to be a prophet of the sixth century BCE (Dan 1:1–8). He makes predictions relating to the second century BCE. (See chapter 11.) The problem is there is a vast consensus among biblical scholars that the book of Daniel was actually written in the second century BCE. My Bible, *The Jerusalem Bible*, a product of the Roman Catholic Church, claims the book was written between 167 and 164 BCE.

The author of Daniel lied about when he wrote the book to enhance his credibility as a prophet. He looks really good. What he writes about in the second century BCE actually happened. The problem is the author of Daniel was not predicting the future but writing history and thus deceiving the people with his prophetic claims. The fraudulent nature of the book of Daniel creates problems for the Christian belief in the second coming of Jesus, a topic we will examine in greater detail in chapter 4.

THE NORTH/SOUTH DIVIDE

The second factor pertaining to historical context is the north/south divide. The starting point is to examine the history and culture of Judea, home of the southern tribes of Israel, and Galilee, where the northern tribes resided. According to Richard Horsley in *Galilee: History, Politics, People*, the history and culture of these two provinces in ancient Israel couldn't be more different. The two provinces were united under the reigns of David and Solomon, but following Solomon's death in 931 BCE the northern tribes in Galilee broke away to form their own state. They remained independent until conquered by Assyria in 722 BCE, which was followed with domination by Persians, Ptolemies, and Seleucids. Eventually Galilee was conquered by the Hasmoneans, the Judean temple-state that came into power in 167 BCE, which again placed the people of Galilee under the control of Judea. However, Judean control only lasted until the Romans came in 63 BCE. As is evident from this history, Galilee and Judea had separate historical existences for virtually all of the time from the death of Solomon to the destruction of the temple in 70 CE.

Unlike Judea, the villages of Galilee had no central institution like the temple to unite them. The temple in Jerusalem was remote from their lives, a five-day walk away, and a source of bitterness because of the taxes imposed during periods of Judean domination. Again, in contrast to Judea, the Galilean tribes lacked a landed aristocracy and sacred scriptures written by historians hired by a king. Galilee was a land of tiny villages and free landowners who tilled the soil. An independent spirit developed among the many tiny villages that was fostered by a rugged mountain terrain and the long distance from a navigable waterway, which made

Background Considerations

communication and trade difficult. Villages were isolated, and economies were self-sufficient, with little money changing hands.[1]

Judea couldn't have been more different. It had a rigid class system with a small upper class made up of priests associated with the temple as well as wealthy landowners and merchants. The vast majority of the population worked as craftsmen building the temple or the gaudy palaces of the rich. They also worked as tent makers, weavers, tailors, cobblers, bakers, and innkeepers servicing Jewish pilgrims coming to Jerusalem for the three main annual festivals. The one thing very few were employed at was tilling the soil. The mountainous terrain and lack of water meant that almost all of the food had to be imported.[2]

These significant differences led to contrasting worldviews, which may help to explain some of the teachings of Jesus. While both societies were male dominant, the status of women differed greatly between them. Women were virtual prisoners in Jerusalem, with their faces hidden by a veil and the prohibitions against their participation in civic life. In the tiny villages of Galilee, women worked alongside their husbands, with faces uncovered, and they were allowed to attend all civic functions, although they could not hold an office. Jesus was known to have had several close female followers, a unique situation for a first-century spiritual leader, which may be explained by his Galilean heritage.

The attitude toward the Torah differed considerably between the two regions. The temple-state in Jerusalem emphasized the laws of Moses pertaining to purity and ritual, those laws which reinforced the legitimacy of the temple. Rural Galileans paid little attention to laws pertaining to purity. Instead, these Galileans focused on the section of Torah relating to economic and social justice. As Jesus railed out against his favorite target, the Pharisees:

> Alas for you scribes and Pharisees, you hypocrites! You pay your tithe of mint and dill and cummin and have neglected the weightier matters of the law—justice, mercy, good faith. (Matt 23:23)

1. Horsley, *Galilee: History, Politics, People*.
2. Jeremias, *Jerusalem in the Time of Jesus*.

The most fascinating difference between the two cultures relates to their contrasting attitudes toward kingship. We assume the coming of a Messiah to rescue Israel was a prominent idea held throughout Israel, but it was primarily a Judean hope. David was not a hero for Galileans. Moses was their man. David and Solomon were both deeply resented by Galileans because of the taxes imposed on them to pay for their wars and building projects. Galileans were also enslaved to work on those projects.

There is an important debate in 1 Samuel about whether Israel should have a king. In chapter 8, both God and Samuel oppose a king, arguing that only Yahweh could be king, a position with wide support in Galilee. (See 1 Sam 8:4-8 and 8:11-18.) In chapter 9, God changes his mind and supports the establishment of a monarchy to protect Israel from the Philistines. (See 1 Sam 9:16-17 and 10:24.) This second position from 1 Samuel on the monarchy reflects the opinions of the temple elite in Jerusalem. Jesus' favorite prophet, Isaiah, agreed with the Galileans on the question of a king, arguing that only Yahweh can be king. (See Isa 43:15, 44:6, and 52:7.)

A careful reading of Jesus' teachings on the subject in the Synoptic Gospels indicates he was true to his Galilean heritage. According to Luke (4:43-44), proclaiming the kingdom of God was what Jesus was sent to do. The key passages in the Lord's prayer on the subject (Matt 6:9-10) tell us that God will bring in the kingdom. You do not pray for the messiah or the Son of Man to come, but for the kingdom of God to arrive, a place where God will rule. The parable of the seed growing secretly (Mark 4:26-29) is about the coming kingdom. Note that no messiah is involved. It's not about liberation through military action by a king or important general, but the mysterious action of God.

THE FIRST-CENTURY WORLDVIEW

Another important factor to consider with regard to Christian Gospel writing is the way in which ancients looked at their world. The Gospel writers saw the world very differently than we do. For

Background Considerations

these writers, the earth was flat, with heaven as a physical place. Stars were viewed as windows through which God peeked out at us humans. Mountains put you closer to God; clouds hid the divine presence. If one was planning to sin, it was best to do it on a cloudy night when God was unable to witness it. We will see examples of this worldview throughout this discussion. One good example, however, comes from Matthew's story of the transfiguration.

> He [Peter] was still speaking when suddenly a bright cloud covered them with a shadow, and from the cloud there came a voice which said, "This is my Son, the Beloved; he enjoys my favor. Listen to him." (Matt 17:5)

The cloud hid the presence of God, a mystery Jews always wanted to protect, but the revelation occurred on a mountain, a setting that placed the recipients of the revelation closer to God.

In addition, ancients had no idea the universe was governed by laws of nature. Instead, God held the whole thing together. As such, God sends or withholds rain, calms seas, brings storms, opens and closes wombs, causes crops to grow, heals disease. Not surprisingly, Jews in first-century Palestine saw Israel as the center of the universe.

These Jews and early Christians also saw the world as being inhabited by tangible spirits. Demons represented Satan or the power of evil. Angels were forces supporting God. These spirit forces challenged each other. The New Testament depicts a battle between God and Satan for control of the universe. The realm between the earth and the moon was seen as the place where these spirits "hung out." A person who could command demons was seen as having divine power. There were lots of people believed to have such power, Jesus among them.

A good example of this spirit saturated worldview is the understanding of disease, which was seen as being caused by evil forces invading the body. Ancients had no idea of the biological causes of disease. When Jesus healed disease, he was defeating the forces of evil, defeating Satan, not dealing with the biological processes we moderns associate with the cause of disease. We will look more closely at this worldview when we examine the miracle stories in chapter 5. To whet your appetite for such a discussion, consider this example from Luke.

> One Sabbath day he was teaching in one of the synagogues, and a woman was there who for eighteen years had been possessed by a spirit that left her enfeebled; she was bent double and quite unable to stand upright. When Jesus saw her, he called over and said, "Woman, you are rid of your infirmity," and he laid his hands on her. And at once she straightened up, and she glorified God. And this woman, a daughter of Abraham whom Satan has held bound these eighteen years—was it not right to untie her bonds on the Sabbath day? (Luke 13:10–13, 16)

Finally, people living in the ancient world were steeped in the supernatural. Holy men, philosophers, great political leaders were often seen as divine men. A divine man was one in whom god's presence was actively present. These people were believed to have been born as a result of divine intervention and to have ascended to heaven following their death. They routinely performed healing miracles, proof that god was working through them. Examples include King Osiris from Egypt. From Greece we have Dionysus, Hercules, Aristaeus, and Asclepius. From Rome, to name a few, we have Aeneas, Romulus, Augustus, and Alexander the Great. In the next section, we will see how the writers of the Gospels describe Jesus using this model.

CHARACTERISTICS OF ANCIENT BIOGRAPHIES

When most Christians hear the word "gospel," they think of book, a biography of Jesus. Instead, the term is defined as a message of good news. The word was first used in the Old Testament to proclaim the birth of a king. In the New Testament, the term "gospel" proclaims the good news of the coming of Jesus, the Messiah. The four Gospels were written to awaken and strengthen faith in Jesus as the Christ, the Greek word for "messiah."

Background Considerations

The Gospels were assembled as a collection of four around 125 CE. They average in length between eleven thousand and nineteen thousand words, a length that was dictated by a need to fit a manuscript on an ancient scroll. Originally the Gospels came without names. Names were eventually added at the end of the second century to enhance the credibility of the work and to distinguish between them. Because only 3 to 5 percent of the population was literate, the Gospels were written primarily for oral presentation. Gifted storytellers in the ancient world were treated much like movie stars today. We will learn how these storytellers created the essential content of the Gospels in the pages that follow.

For years a debate has taken place in the scholarly community as to whether the Gospels were unique in ancient literature or part of a larger genre of ancient biography. Today that debate has largely been won by those who argue the Gospels are a type of Greek/Roman biography, a laudatory biography whose purpose was to show the greatness of a person.[3]

Although there are many differences among Greco-Roman biographies, they all share a similar mythical worldview. In the case of the Synoptic Gospels of Matthew, Mark, and Luke, the model is that of the divine man of Hellenistic culture. Remember that the Gospels were written in Greek by Hellenistic Jews who were well schooled in that culture.

These Hellenistic Jews believed Jesus was a holy man, the Jewish Messiah, the savior for all those who believed in him. As a result, they placed in their Gospels stories that made that point, stories that pictured Jesus as a divine man, stories about a miraculous birth, stories of Jesus the miracle worker, and stories of Jesus' ascension to heaven following the crucifixion.[4]

Within this genre of ancient literature, there are many biographies of holy sages written to fit the divine man model. In the last section, I listed several of these sages from Egypt, Greece, and Rome. Many of the stories of these men sound very similar to ones about Jesus in the four Gospels.

---

3. See Talbert, *What Is a Gospel?*; and Burridge, *What Are the Gospels?*
4. Talbert, *What Is a Gospel?*, 25–38.

The mythological worldview of John is somewhat different. The writer of John portrays a savior who comes from heaven, takes on a human form, and returns to heaven. Again, the model comes from Greco-Roman mythology of descending/ascending gods who appear on earth for creation and redemption purposes.[5]

These gods while appearing on earth act as intermediaries for the god in heaven. The *logos* figure as described by Philo, the first-century Jewish philosopher from Egypt, is a mediator who comes to earth from God to establish a link between the hidden mystery of God and human beings.[6] This logos figure is featured in the Prologue in John (1:1–18).

Ancient biographies have little in common with modern biographies. Ancient biographers were not interested in looks, family life, education, or personality. Neither were these authors concerned about developmental factors, i.e., those forces that shaped the individual under study. Few were organized chronologically from birth to death. Ancient biographies were about the finished product. What did the person do? An important focus was on public deeds. They were also interested in character. What made the person great? What character traits were worthy of moral emulation? Finally, what did the person say? Was he a teacher of ethics, and did he leave behind a collection of his teachings?[7]

The four Gospels exhibit these characteristics. They do differ from many ancient biographies in that they have a missionary purpose. The Gospels were written to create faith.[8] In no way, however, did the Gospel writers think they were writing sacred scripture. They were writing in praise of their hero and to answer questions raised in their communities.

Typical elements within these biographies include a collection of episodes. All four Gospels have this feature. Another common element was the inclusion of travel narratives like we find in Luke and Acts. Birth stories were popular as Matthew and Luke

---

5. Talbert, *What Is a Gospel?*, 53–55.
6. Talbert, *What Is a Gospel?*, 56–63.
7. Burridge, *What Are the Gospels?*
8. Aune, *New Testament in Its Literary Environment*, 5.

attest. Almost without exception ancient biographies included stories about the death of the person in question.[9]

Plausibility was the primary test for separating fact from falsehood. Jesus was believed to be a divine man, and as a result miracle stories about him were plausible. Ancient people expected such stories.[10]

Our final characteristic of ancient biographies is the problem of reliable historical data. There was little of it. There were no reporters or TV cameras following these people around. Few records were kept, and few letters were available for use by the biographer. Ancient biographies were often written long after the events. Stories about the Buddha were not written down until five hundred years after his death; with Confucius the lag time was two hundred years. As a result, the stories in these biographies were most often fictional accounts; however, as we will see with the four Gospels, these fictional stories were written to convey important truths the creators believed pertained to the person under study.

SOURCES OF STORY CREATION

As I have pointed out throughout these introductory topics, problems of the absence of reliable historical data have affected the writing of the New Testament. While the Gospel of Mark was only written forty years after the death of Jesus, the big problem was the Jewish/Roman War from 66–73 CE. As a result of Rome's destruction of Jerusalem, hard historical data was lost, which left the oral tradition as an important source of Gospel material.[11]

Stories about Jesus were not originally written down. Instead, they were passed down by word of mouth for forty years before they were collected and placed in the Gospel of Mark. Many of

9. Aune, *New Testament in Its Literary Environment*, 46–66.

10. Aune, *New Testament in Its Literary Environment*, 64.

11. The discussion that follows on the oral tradition is well known within the scholarly community. I am especially indebted to Ehrman, *Jesus Before the Gospels*; Crossan, *Birth of Christianity*; McKnight, *What Is Form Criticism?*; and Schmidt, *Framework of the Jesus Story*.

these stories did not come as fully developed narratives but in short, independent units, called pericopes. A story may have been initiated from historical memory, but as it was passed along the oral tradition highway the author of the story soon lost control. Changes were inevitable. Think of the telephone game with people sitting in a circle whispering rumors to a friend beside them.

These units or pericopes come with little attention to context or chronology. Jesus is driven by the Holy Spirit to the desert in Mark (1:13). He gives a major presentation of his teachings on a mountain in Matthew (5:1). Note that in both cases no additional details related to context are provided, with the result that you have no idea regarding the time, day, or place where the event actually took place. When details of context are provided, they are often highly incomplete as is evident in the two geographical locations in Mark. (See Mark 5:1 and 10:1.) As these two examples attest, the appearance of context is provided; however, when looked at closely, the reader has little idea where the event described in the story actually took place.

The four Gospels are in part a chain of these units neatly organized and stitched together. These units moved along the oral tradition highway by being performed and preached. The more the stories were told and retold, the more they changed. Synagogues were a main repository for them. The method of presentation affected their transmission. Performers make material their own. Because there was rarely a written script for Jesus stories, there were lots of possibilities for these stories to change as they were performed to different audiences and by different storytellers. In synagogues (the setting), preachers added drama for effect. The point of these early sermons was not the life of Jesus, but Jesus the savior of the world. Deeds were used to support a messianic claim, but the purpose was never biography as we understand it. First-century preachers also had no interest in objectivity. Their goal was to persuade.

The stories handed down via the oral tradition had to be remembered. There was no taping system in first-century Palestine.

Background Considerations

Memory is a tricky process. People in the first century did not have better memories than we moderns.

People remember what they want to remember. You remember the dramatic, often forgetting the details. Memory is a reconstructive process that blends together fact, imagination, and desire. Desire is an important organizing mechanism for the human brain. We cannot process data objectively because there is too much of it. As a result, we select out what we want to remember. This process creates bias.[12]

As I mentioned above, stories about Jesus were passed down without context and with many details missing. There was rarely information about time or place for an event. When details are forgotten, performers make them up so that a seamless story can be presented. It's a process that can easily lead to invention where one imagines something that over time becomes fact. It's a process that does not produce what we moderns consider to be historical fact.

This process allowed the final editor a great deal of freedom in creating his stories about Jesus. There was a large tradition (collection of stories) to choose from. In Mark, the first Gospel written, Jesus has a one-year ministry, which ends with a climactic week in Jerusalem. The final editor who put together John chose differently from the oral tradition. In John's Gospel, Jesus has a three-year ministry, with his last stay in Jerusalem lasting six months. There are also no parables in John, no exorcisms, and the miracle stories, with two exceptions, are original to him. To repeat what was said above, the editor of John chose very differently from the oral tradition than the three evangelists from the synoptic tradition.

Final editors often embellished the stories they inherited. Mark (6:1-6) tells the story of Jesus' first sermon in Nazareth. Luke (4:16-30) uses this story but more than doubles the length by adding two stories about Elijah and Elisha. These add-ons are only found in Luke. When stories are unique to a Gospel, it often signals an important theological point the Gospel writer wants to make. When we examine Luke in chapter 4, you will see this was

---

12. See Crossan, *Birth of Christianity*, 59–68. See also Damasio, *Descartes' Error*; and Le Doux, *Synoptic Self.*

the case. Storytellers were also known to make the material more dramatic. The story in Mark (chapter 5) where Jesus exorcises a demon from a long-suffering man is a good case in point. After exorcising the demon, Jesus proceeds to send the evil spirits into a herd of pigs. Pigs, for Jews, were unclean animals. This act, almost certainly not historical, would have played well among first-century Jews. It would also be a story they would remember.

Stories of deeds allegedly performed by Jesus were passed along through the oral tradition. The cleansing of the temple is a good example. This dramatic act by Jesus is the type of action that would most likely be remembered. It is reported in all four Gospels, which makes it likely to have happened. What is interesting is the cleansing of the temple comes at the end of Mark's Gospel (11:15-19) and is used to explain the arrest of Jesus. Matthew and Luke follow Mark in this regard. John describes the same event at the beginning of his Gospel (2:13-20) and uses it to make the point that Jesus is creating a new religion. This example illustrates again that stories moved along the oral tradition highway without context, without a clear understanding of the time and place where the event took place. This enabled the storyteller to use the event for his own purpose in story creation.

The same situation exists with the Sanhedrin meeting held by Jewish leaders to condemn Jesus.[13] Mark has it as a trial with Jesus in attendance during the last week of his life. After hearing the evidence against Jesus, the high priest proclaims he deserves to die (14:53-65). In John, the event is portrayed as a meeting of Jewish leaders who are afraid of Jesus' increasing popularity with the people (11:45-54). Jesus is not in attendance. The decision is made to kill him. The meeting takes place several weeks before the Passover celebration.

There are additional examples of deeds of Jesus in different places and used for different purposes in the four Gospels. What these examples show is that the oral tradition comes in discrete, independent units, with no context. Storytellers creatively chose

---

13. The Sanhedrin was the main Jewish governing body in Jerusalem. It had both legislative and judicial powers.

Background Considerations

from among these deeds to create their stories of Jesus. The authors add details and context to make the stories understandable and to flow seamlessly within their Gospel.

The oral tradition encourages final editors to organize their portrayal of Jesus by story type, not chronology. These editors gather together parables, miracles stories, conflict stories, stories of exorcisms, and Jesus' teachings, and then place them within a collection of similar stories in their Gospel. Transitions between each of the stories within the collection are invented by the Gospel writer.

A good example of this practice is found in Matthew's story of the Sermon on the Mount. Note that no clear sense of context for place is given. Matthew places it on a mountain (5:1). Most scholars argue that the editor of Matthew invented the idea of a sermon as a device to present a summary of Jesus' teachings. He collected these teachings from the oral tradition and presented them together in a sermon. As I will demonstrate in chapter 3, the discourses in Matthew on missionary teachings, parables, and church life were written in the same way.

Mark's Gospel also illustrates this process. Mark 1:23—2:12 includes a number of cures. Mark 2:15-28 reports a collection of conflict stories between Jesus and the Jewish establishment. The parables are found in chapter 4, verses 1-34. Two nature miracle stories occur in 6:30-52, and Jesus' ethical teachings are summarized in chapter 10, verses 1-31.

A central problem with the oral tradition is that it can't get us back to the historical Jesus. As I indicated above, the confrontation at the temple probably happened, but when—at the beginning of Jesus' ministry or at the end? All four Gospels report that Jesus was a miracle worker. Josephus, the first-century Jewish historian, describes Jesus as a miracle worker, which gives this fact about him historical credibility because he was not a follower of Jesus. The problem is that history can only confirm Jesus' reputation as a miracle worker. It cannot go back and evaluate specific stories of Jesus' healing miracles to confirm or deny their historical credibility. Information regarding day, time, and place are not available.

It was a long journey from the original words of Jesus in Aramaic to their being written down in Greek. Unfortunately, there is little one can do to study the process of transmission along the oral tradition highway because nothing was written down in the early stages of transmission. Written collections of these stories came later. We know nothing about Jewish synagogues where members of the Jesus movement gathered in Palestine prior to the Jewish/Roman War where stories about Jesus were most certainly told. No evidence of a written Aramaic tradition has survived. The oral tradition begins and ends in the Hellenistic world toward the last third of the first century. We cannot get back to Palestine during the time of Jesus in order to see the original version of a story. The fact that this oral tradition was the most important source of stories about Jesus tells us quite emphatically the Gospels are not based on history as we know it.

On the other hand, the existence of this oral tradition is remarkable. Where there is smoke there is fire. For an oral tradition to survive, people have to be intensely interested in it. Jesus must have had an amazing impact on the people he came in contact with. Stories about him survived the Great War and the relocation of the Jesus movement in the Hellenistic world. He must have done some amazing things. The sad fact, however, is that it is very difficult to get back to accurate specifics. Those details have been lost.

Jewish sacred scripture was also an important source of story creation. The Old Testament was "in the head" of both storytellers and Gospel writers. When something about Jesus triggered their memory of an Old Testament story, they used it to fill in details from stories that came up from the oral tradition. This was seen as legitimate because Gospel writers believed the Old Testament was all about Jesus, the Messiah.

The story of Jesus' triumphant entry into Jerusalem (Mark 11:1–10) on a colt with some people spreading their coats on the road and others spreading greenery cut from their fields is a case in point. The story was inspired by Zech 9:9. Read it. Mark chooses this passage in Zechariah because the king in the story is meek and gentle, reminding him of Jesus. He rides into Jerusalem on a colt

Background Considerations

rather than a war horse. He established his kingdom peacefully. The words of the crowd in Mark's story were most likely taken from Ps 118.

> Hosanna! Blessings on him who comes in the name of the Lord. (Mark 11:10)
>
> Blessings on him who comes in the name of Yahweh! (Ps 118:26)

This story in Mark is most likely fiction, a story created by the editor to make a point about Jesus, the Messiah. Because he believed the Old Testament was all about Jesus, the story in Zechariah about a king who was humble and who would bring peace to Israel must be a story about Jesus. Why do we suspect the story was fictional? Remember, this was Passover—a celebration of the freeing of the Israelites from Egyptian colonial rule. Many Jews in first-century Palestine were waiting for God to repeat that miracle. The Romans were on edge, with many additional troops deployed to protect against troublemakers during the festival. There was only one road into Jerusalem. It only makes common sense to imagine Roman soldiers patrolling that road. If Jesus had in fact entered Jerusalem on a colt with enthusiastic crowd support proclaiming him a king, the Romans would have arrested him on the spot.

This point is reinforced in Matthew's version of the story (21:1–11). According to Matthew, as Jesus enters the city, Jerusalem is in turmoil (21:10). There is no way Rome would have allowed such an entry under those conditions.

It is also important to note that only Jesus was crucified. If he had really entered Jerusalem as a king, thus posing a significant political threat, Rome would have gone after his disciples too. Close political followers of a king would also have been seen as a problem. The key to understanding Jesus' death was his attack on the temple. That confrontation threatened the power and status of the Jewish religious establishment, not Roman colonial rule. It was these Jewish leaders who convinced Pilate to crucify Jesus. The disciples were not seen as a problem. With their teacher gone, they would return to their homes in Galilee.

A second example comes from 2 Kgs 4:42–44. There Elisha feeds one hundred men with twenty barley loaves, with bread left over. All four Gospels report the story of Jesus feeding five thousand stranded followers with five barley loaves, with bread left over. God's work in the past was believed to predict the future. The Gospel writers also wanted to make the point that Jesus was greater than Elisha. He fed five thousand. When we discuss the miracle stories in chapter 5, you will see that many of Jesus' miracles were patterned on Old Testament models.

A final example of the use of the Old Testament for story creation comes from Matthew's virgin birth story. Rumors have persisted for centuries that Jesus' birth was not legitimate. One of these rumors involves a Roman soldier named Pantera. The Gemara, a later collection of commentaries on the Talmud, makes such a reference to Pantera as the father of Jesus.[14] Although we do not know the precise date in which Jesus was born, it is quite likely he was born during the occupation of Nazareth by the Roman army during their siege of Sepphoris in 4 BCE. Sepphoris was located three miles from Nazareth and was in a state of rebellion against Roman colonial rule. Jewish women were known to have been forced to service Roman soldiers. It is therefore possible that Mary was forced into such a situation, which led to the birth of Jesus. The Gemara references are slim evidence, but it's the only evidence we have regarding the birth of Jesus with the exception of the two fictional accounts in Matthew and Luke, a topic we will examine in detail in chapter 4.

Returning to the New Testament, hints of such a possibility appear in Mark's Gospel when Jesus returns to preach his first sermon at Nazareth. The people of Nazareth were astonished when he spoke and said, "This is the carpenter, surely, the son of Mary" (6:3). The designation "son of Mary" is a strange one in a patriarchal society where children were universally known by their father.

Bishop Spong speculates in *Biblical Literalism: A Gentile Heresy* that Matthew creates his genealogy to defend the birth of Jesus. The genealogy (Matt 1:2–16) dates back eighteen hundred years.

---

14. See Wilson, *Jesus: A Life*, 67; and Ehrman, *Did Jesus Exist?*, 76.

Background Considerations

Obviously, this genealogy was not based on historic records that did not exist; and, if you compare it with Luke's genealogy (3:23–38), there are no parallels. What is interesting is the list in Matthew includes four gentile women, all with discredited sexual pasts. These four women from Jesus' line are Tamar, a prostitute from Judah, Rahab, a prostitute for the city of Jericho, Ruth, a seductress, and Bathsheba, the woman David seduced who became the mother of Solomon. By linking Jesus to these four women, Matthew suggests God can create something holy from a discredited past. The author uses the Old Testament to help make this point.

The Old Testament solved an important data problem for New Testament storytellers and Gospel writers. Because of the total destruction of Jerusalem in 70 CE where the Jesus movement was headquartered, reliable historical evidence regarding the life and ministry of Jesus was lost. Gospel storytellers used the Old Testament to fill in missing details in stories passed along the oral tradition highway.

Prior to 70 CE, however, a sense that Jesus remained as a living presence was held by his closest followers. Because of his continued presence with them, his closest followers came to believe that Jesus was alive in some way. Over time they concluded he was alive in heaven as God's special agent, the Son of Man. As a result, they reinterpreted the Jewish messiah concept along the lines of the Daniel prophecy.

As Christian churches emerged in the Hellenistic world following the crucifixion and especially after the destruction of Jerusalem, members of these early congregations had many questions regarding the identity of Jesus. Christian storytellers provided the answers. These storytellers were filled with the spirit of Jesus, his continuing presence with them, and convinced that he was the promised Jewish Messiah reconfigured as the Son of Man. Lacking hard historical evidence and believing that Jewish scripture was all about God's promised messiah, it was natural for them to turn to the Old Testament for inspiration in creating their stories. This was the ancient way. Fictional stories were created to express important truths held by storytellers who had little historical data to guide them.

2

The Gospel of Mark

GOSPEL MECHANICS

TO BEGIN WITH, WE have no idea who the author of Mark was or where the Gospel was written. There are some theories claiming the place of writing was Rome and the author was John Mark, the interpreter of Peter; but this theory and others like it are nothing more than speculation. Let me make one brief comment with regard to the John Mark theory. The picture of Peter presented in Mark is scathing. Peter never understands who Jesus is and denies him three times. It is very unlikely the author of Mark got his information from a close associate of Peter.

Very few scholars today believe that any of the Gospels were written by eyewitnesses to the events of Jesus' life and ministry. No Gospels claim to be written by eyewitnesses. There are no statements in any of the four Gospels that went something like "I was with Jesus when . . . ." In addition, the most obvious eyewitnesses were the disciples, who were illiterate peasants. There is no way illiterate peasants whose native language was Aramaic could have written Gospels in Greek. The average lifespan of a male living in first-century Palestine was thirty years. It is highly unlikely male eyewitnesses were alive forty years after the crucifixion when Mark was believed to have been written. Such an eyewitness would have had to survive the Great War and to have lived well beyond the average lifespan of a male in the first century. Finally, the four evangelists were unfamiliar with the geography of Palestine and the operation of Jewish institutions, suggesting quite strongly they were not natives of Galilee or Jerusalem.

With regards to Mark, examples of his mistakes regarding Palestinian geography are found throughout his Gospel. In the story where Jesus returns to Nazareth to preach his first sermon (6:1–2), he speaks in the synagogue. Archaeologists who have researched this issue have determined that no synagogue existed in Nazareth until the third century of the Common Era.[1] In Mark 8:10, Jesus gets into a boat with his disciples, and they proceed to Dalmanutha. No such place exists, both then or now. The journey from Tyre to Sidon through the Decapolis is hard to figure out. (See Mark 7:31.) Finally, there is a problem in the story where the disciples of Jesus deny him three times and the rooster crows. Roosters were not allowed in Jerusalem according to Jewish law. No Palestinian Jew or eyewitness to the events would have made the mistakes described above. Later in the chapter, when we examine the passion narrative in detail, you will see how Mark was confused regarding the operation of the Sanhedrin, the chief legislative/judicial institution in first-century Palestine.

With regard to the author of Mark, I will conclude at the end of the chapter that the Gospel was not written by one author, but rather was created by a process that began with the oral performances of three gifted storytellers. Eventually an editor produced a written copy of those performances, almost certainly not the original ones, and the Gospel of Mark attained written form. The written version we have in the New Testament came one hundred years after the stories first received written form. During the one hundred year interval between the first written text and the one we now possess, scribes copied texts and made changes they deemed to be appropriate. Chapter 5 will demonstrate this process in much greater detail.

---

1. Crossan and Reed, *Excavating Jesus*, 25–26.

For the date of writing, there is a general consensus that this process began around 70 CE. I say process because I will point out in what follows there are three main stories presented in Mark. The original version of the first story about the coming of the kingdom of God most likely came into existence before 70 CE.[2] The second story about the rejection of the Jews makes allusions to the war with Rome and the burning of Jerusalem in 70 CE in chapter 13 of the Gospel. It could easily have attained written form after 70. The elements of the third story, the passion narrative, most likely appeared before 70 CE.

Scholars have noted there was no interest in the circumcision debate in Mark's Gospel. This controversy raged in the 50s when Paul was writing. The controversy centered around the terms for admitting gentiles into the Jesus movement. Was it necessary for them to become Jews first before converting to Christianity? The fact that you do not see mention of this controversy in Mark suggests the different parts of the Gospel were written after the 50s, a time when the circumcision controversy for most Christians had been resolved.

Mark is written in a popular Greek style. I loved it when I first read the Gospel in Greek fifty-five years ago. The version we have in the New Testament uses simple, declarative sentences. The pace is fast moving. The writer is excited. You can sense it. The time is fulfilled. The kingdom of God is at hand.

The final editor obviously loved threes. There are three seed parables, three opinions of John the Baptist, three boat scenes, three predictions of Jesus' passion, three discussions of the failure of Jesus' disciples to remain awake at Gethsemane, and three denials by Peter. Obviously, this is not history, but a literary device to make an impression on people to help them remember. The vast majority of people in the first century would be exposed to Mark through oral presentation and would not be able to look back at text to refresh their memories.

---

2. I say the original version for the first story because, as you will soon see, representatives of the early church added material pertaining to the Son of Man at a later date.

The Gospel of Mark

In the last chapter, it was argued that stories moved along the oral tradition highway with little attention to time or place. Take a look at Mark 4:11 through Mark 5:43. The story begins with Jesus preaching among the people in the late afternoon. He then sails to the land of the Gerasenes where he heals a demoniac (5:1). From there he sails back to the other side of the lake to heal Jairus's daughter. All this takes place in one day, the logistics of which could not be accomplished in a twenty-four-hour span. With regard to place, the Spirit drives Jesus into the desert (1:13), a rather large place with no specific location given. He calls his first disciples along the lake in Galilee (1:16). Again, the story lacks a specific location. The transfiguration occurs on a high mountain (9:2). Mark selected stories based on their content with no interest in chronology or location.

The editor took stories from the oral tradition, organized them, invented context, and added details to create a seamless story. This was a very creative task. He posited a one-year ministry for Jesus, which is probably not historical. Most scholars prefer John's arrangement, which describes a three-year ministry. Scholarly arguments supporting John's position are complicated. The best one argues the Jesus portrayed in the Synoptics, the Gospels based on Mark's one-year organization scheme, seems to have been in Jerusalem before the last week of the Passover festival. He seems to know the person who loans him the colt (Mark 11: 1–5) and the owner of the house where the Last Supper is held (Mark 14:12–16).

There is a general agreement among scholars that Mark was the first of the four New Testament Gospels to attain written form. The evidence for this conclusion is impressive. To begin with, Matthew and Luke improve Mark's grammar, provide better transitions linking stories, and correct his obvious mistakes. An interesting example of the latter comes from the passion narrative. When Jesus is before the Sanhedrin, Mark reports that all members vote to condemn him to death (14:64). This creates a problem because Joseph of Arimathaea is both a member of the Sanhedrin and a known follower of Jesus (15:43). Matthew keeps the verdict unanimous (26:66) but takes Joseph out of the Sanhedrin (27:58).

Luke solves the problem by having Joseph vote against the verdict (22:51). The decision is no longer unanimous.

Mark has a very distinctive style of storytelling. Many stories appear in the form of an oreo cookie. Nine stories proceed in this fashion. Event A is introduced, the outer layer of chocolate for the cookie. Event B is then interjected and told as a complete story—the white stuff of the cookie. The story in event A is then completed, making the second layer of outer chocolate.

Read the story of the bringing back to life of Jairus's daughter (5:21–43). In event A, the daughter of Jairus is introduced as desperately sick. Event B describes the cure of the woman with a hemorrhage as a complete story. The story of Jairus's daughter who Jesus brings back to life, event A, is now completed. As I mention above, Mark has nine of these stories. There are five in Matthew, four in Luke. If Matthew was the first Gospel written and Mark was dependent on it, the question becomes, Where did Mark get the additional four stories? This discrepancy is easier to explain if Mark comes first. In this case, Matthew chooses to omit four of Mark's oreo structured stories. With regard to an important theme in this book, Mark's oreo technique makes for good storytelling—it helps to illustrate the main event in A—but it is not good history.

In addition to Matthew and Luke's corrections, Mark's stories are shorter. Matthew and Luke add details, sometimes lots of details. We have noted this point with Jesus' first sermon in Nazareth. Compare Mark 6:1–6 and Luke 4:16–30. Finally, scholars point out that if Matthew was first, as most people originally believed, and Mark copied from him, why does Mark omit the virgin birth story and the Sermon on the Mount?

THE COMING KINGDOM OF GOD

The Gospel of Mark is organized around three stories—the coming kingdom of God, God's rejection of the Jews, and the passion narrative. In chapter 1 of Mark's Gospel, Jesus begins his ministry following the arrest of John the Baptist. His first act is to declare the kingdom of God is close at hand. He then proceeds to heal disease and exorcise demons. With these acts, we learn the kingdom of God is coming to the land of Israel.

The storyteller describes a world in chaos because Satan is in control. Human bodies are diseased because Satan has invaded them. People are demon possessed, a sign of Satan's control over their personality. Storms at sea are the result of Satan stirring the waters.

At Jesus' baptism he is empowered by the Holy Spirit to battle Satan. Immediately following the baptism he is led into the desert, the place where Satan was believed to reside, to do battle (1:9–13). This is war. Jesus empowers his disciples to join the battle, and they too travel Israel healing the sick and casting out demons (6:7–13). It is a battle to save the land of Israel, and Jesus is winning. He is destroying the power of Satan. The tone is urgent. The action is fast paced. The word "immediately" appears throughout the first eight chapters.

The storyteller creates this story by selectively choosing episodes from the oral tradition where Jesus heals a disease by defeating Satan. One healing episode follows another in these early chapters. The same is the case for exorcisms. The parables in chapter 4 indicate that the kingdom is for the land of Israel, and they provide pictures of what the kingdom would be like (4:1–32).

Selecting discrete, episodic stories from a written collection of like stories to create a larger story was a common technique used by storytellers and Gospel writers. The goal was to create a vivid picture that could be easily remembered by the listening audience. In this case, the picture created by the storyteller was of Jesus battling Satan to bring God's kingdom to Israel. Ancient society was an oral culture. The literacy rate was no higher than 5 percent. This story would be performed over and over again before attaining written form as part of Mark's Gospel.[3]

The coming of God's kingdom raises one of the most challenging questions in the New Testament; namely, was this kingdom to be located in Israel for Jews or in heaven for gentiles? The analysis above indicates that the original story in Mark locates

---

3. See Dewey, *Oral Ethos of the Early Church*.

the kingdom in Israel. Satan controlled the land of Israel, and Jesus was defeating him so that God's kingdom could emerge. The confusion comes because a scribe or a final editor from the first-century church has inserted several Son of Man statements into the Gospel which suggest otherwise, that the kingdom would be for gentiles in heaven.

Who is this Son of Man? This figure was first described in Dan 7:13 as a transcendent, preexistent, heavenly being. He was further developed in 1 En 45–71 and 4 Ezra 13:1–53. The preexistent part means that he was with God from the beginning of time. However, the Son of Man is not understood as God's equal, as the Son of God in traditional Christian Trinitarian belief. Rather the Son of Man is God's divine agent who will judge the world and bring the righteous to heaven.

A key event in Mark's Gospel takes place at Caesarea Philippi when Peter declares Jesus to be the Christ (8:29). The problem is that Peter thinks of Jesus as the expected Jewish Messiah, as the king who will lead Israel to greatness; and for that belief, Jesus rebukes Peter. Jesus declares himself to be the Son of Man who would be put to death and after three days rise again (18:31–32).

Jesus is pictured as the Son of Man throughout the Gospel. The title is used to designate the Jesus of history as the Son of Man (Mark 2:10, 2:28, 9:12, 10:45, and 14:21). There are three prophecies of the passion where it is predicted that Jesus as the Son of Man will suffer, be rejected, put to death, and rise to heaven on the third day (Mark 8:31, 9:31, and 10:33). It is important to get Jesus to heaven if he is to return to earth as the Son of Man. Finally, there are three references to a Son of Man who will return from the clouds with great power and glory to gather the elect and take them to heaven (Mark 8:38, 13:26–27, and 14:62).

The Son of Man statements cited above were inserted into the Gospel by the early church. In doing so, church leaders were putting words into Jesus' mouth. That's an amazing claim which needs further explanation.

The clearest example of Gospel writers putting words into Jesus' mouth can be seen in his last words on the cross. Mark is believed to be the primary author of the passion narrative for the Synoptic Gospels. He and Matthew have very similar stories. Both evangelists present Jesus as being abandoned by his followers and God. His prayer is not answered at Gethsemane, and his disciples flee when he is arrested. He faces the cross alone and agonizes over it. His last words before dying in both Gospels are, "My God, my God. Why have you deserted me?" (Mark 15:34 and Matt 27:47).

The picture is different in Luke. In Luke, Jesus appears as a stoic, quietly accepting his fate. He praises his disciples for standing by him (Luke 22:28–30), and his prayer is answered at Gethsemane (Luke 22:44). There are no expressions of anguish in Luke's version of the story. Jesus' last words on the cross are "Father, into your hands I commit my spirit" (Luke 23:46).

With John, the events are different from Mark's listing. John has no triumphant entry into Jerusalem on a colt, no Gethsemane scene, no temple confrontation, and no trial before the Sanhedrin. In John's story, Jesus is pictured as the stage director. He controls the arrest scene where he greets Judas. When he identifies himself to the Roman soldiers, they fall down in awe and reverence. In a real sense, Jesus allows them to arrest him. He dominates the meeting with Pilate. His last words on the cross say it all: "It is accomplished" (John 19:30).

The three brief summaries of the passion narratives in Mark, Luke, and John present three different versions of Jesus' last words on the cross. At minimum two Gospel writers put words into Jesus' mouth. This is a freedom the Gospel writers exercised frequently when writing their Gospel stories as we will see throughout this book.

With the fact that Gospel writers put words into the mouth of Jesus firmly established, we can now turn to the Son of Man statements cited above. We know that these statements did not come from the historical Jesus because they point to an entirely different religion from the one Jesus preached and practiced. Salvation for Jesus was for Jews as a nation in the land of Israel as we see from the original coming of God's kingdom story. Jesus speaks about a kingdom coming, not about his imminent return. Salvation for the early church was brought by the Son of Man who would return to earth as judge and take the righteous to heaven. The religion of the early church has nothing to do with the religion of Jesus. This point will gain greater clarity when we outline the teachings of Jesus in the next chapter.

The idea that the Son of Man statements were inserted into Mark's Gospel by a scribe or final editor also needs explaining. Ancient literary works were often collaborative, not the work of one author. All four Gospels are collaborative efforts. There were no copyright laws in the ancient world protecting authors and the integrity of their work. An author often collaborated with a scribe. He dictated his work. As secretaries, the scribes took great latitude in what they wrote down and often made changes. In a similar way, scribes making an additional copy of a work often made changes in the content of the original work.[4] This new version of the text was copied by scribes when making additional copies at a later date, which gave the new version wide circulation. The written copy we have of Mark didn't appear until the end of the second century, giving this process of textual change many years to work itself out.

There is almost a universal consensus among biblical scholars that the last eleven verses in Mark (16:9-19) were added by a scribe, an issue I will discuss in further detail in the next section. Again, there is a near universal consensus among scholars that the story of the adulterous woman in John (8:2-12) was added by a scribe. The story doesn't appear in the earliest texts we have of John. Read Mark 14:51-52. After Jesus is arrested by a group of armed guards, a young man wearing nothing but a linen cloth runs away. In doing so, the cloth falls from him, and he runs away naked. This silly episode has little to do with the arrest of Jesus and was probably inserted by a scribe who was making a copy of the Gospel.

Unlike that last example, most insertions into a text had a purpose. The one making the insertion had an agenda, a point of view he wanted expressed. In the case of the Son of Man statements inserted into Mark by the first-century church, the intent was to change the understanding of Jesus as the Messiah. He was

---

4. Botha, *Orality and Literacy in Early Christianity*.

no longer the prophet announcing the coming of God's kingdom to Israel. Instead, he became the preexistent Son of Man who would come from heaven to rescue the righteous and take them to heaven.

A storyteller who was convinced Jesus was the expected Messiah created a story using material from the oral tradition to demonstrate how the promised kingdom was coming into existence. Jesus was pictured defeating Satan, which would enable God's rule to emerge. This was a kingdom located in Israel. When Israel as a nation ceased to exist following the Roman invasion (66–73 CE), the story had to be changed. It is interesting that rather than rewrite the story, church leaders just added several Son of Man statements indicating that salvation would now be for individuals in heaven. This is an example of Gospels being written in part by committee, a practice as you will see created much confusion regarding the Jesus story.

THE JEWS REJECTED: A STORY

The first-century Roman world from which the Gospel of Mark emerged was an oral culture. As I have commented several times, fewer than 5 percent of the population could read or write. Storytellers were honored members of the society and played an important role in disseminating information to the general population.

New Testament scholars describe the community for which the Gospel of Mark was written as being primarily gentile based. After the destruction of Jerusalem by the Roman invasion in 70 CE, a significant question became, Why has God rejected the Jews? This is an important question because the central premise of the Jewish religion was that God had chosen the people of Israel to be their exclusive God and had promised to protect them. Here is how the storyteller explained to his gentile community why God has rejected the Jews and salvation was now being given to them.[5]

---

5. This story is well accepted within the scholarly literature on Mark. It was first suggested to me by Ehrman, *New Testament*, 59–68. See also Brown, *Introduction*, 171–224; Burridge, *Four Gospels*; Rhoads, Dewey, and Michie, *Mark*

In the very first verse of the Gospel, Jesus is identified as the Son of God (1:1). Read it. This verse introduces the gospel story. The gentile congregation has heard that Jesus is the Son of God. I will give away a little of the story. No Jew will hear these words or understand this idea throughout the entire Gospel. God has given up on the Jews because they have rejected Jesus as the Messiah.

In the story of Jesus' baptism, the voice announcing Jesus as the Son of God comes from heaven so that God can speak privately to Jesus (1:11). God whispers in his ear, so to speak. The Jews with John the Baptist on the Jordan river in Mark do not hear God proclaim Jesus as his Son.

Matthew softens this idea somewhat. In his version of the story, the voice spoke from heaven. All who were there at the river were able to hear God's declaration. Matthew is not as obsessed with keeping this understanding of Jesus away from Jews. You may see this as silly, but as I will argue throughout this book, small editorial changes can make a significant difference. You don't get just one, but several, and these little changes all point in the same direction.

> And a voice came from heaven, "You are my Son, the Beloved; my favor rests on you." (Mark 1:11)

> And a voice spoke from heaven, "This is my Son, the Beloved; my favor rests on him." (Matt 3:17)

Continuing with chapter 1, we see Jesus healing many who were suffering from disease, and he exorcises several demons. The demons recognize him as the Son of God—spirits understand their spirit enemy—but Jesus doesn't allow them to speak about his identity as Son of God.

> That evening, after sunset, they brought to him all who were sick and those who were possessed by devils. The whole town came crowding around the door, and he cured many who were suffering from diseases of one kind or another; he also cast out many devils, but he

---

as *Story*; Hooker, *Message of Mark*; France, *Gospel of Matthew*; and Kingsbury, *Christology of Mark's Gospel*.

would not allow them to speak because they knew who he was. (Mark 1:32–34; see also Mark 3:10–12)

A leper comes to him, begging on his knees. Jesus feels sorry for him and cures him on the spot. Jesus then sternly warns the man, "Mind you say nothing to anyone" (1:44). This happens time and time again in Mark's Gospel.

In chapter 4, he speaks to the crowd in parables. The idea is for them to listen but not understand. The purpose of these obtuse parables is to hide God's new plan for salvation from the Jews. The author of this story is telling his congregation: Do you see what God did when Jesus was teaching the Jewish crowds? He taught them in parables they couldn't understand. Why? Because God has rejected the Jews and opened salvation for us.

> When he was alone, the Twelve, together with the others who formed his company, asked what the parables meant. He told them, "The secret of the kingdom of God is given to you, but to those who are outside everything comes in parables, so that they may see and see again, but not perceive; may hear and hear again, but not understand; otherwise they might be converted and be forgiven." (Mark 4:10–12)

Can you imagine Jesus acting in such a mean-spirited way? This is story, not history.

In chapter 5, Jesus enters gentile country and heals a man possessed by demons. He sends the demons into a herd of pigs who run into a lake and drown. Jesus tells the man to go home and tell his friends all that God has done for him (5:19). These gentiles from the territory of Gerasenes are allowed to hear the good news of Jesus, the son of God.

In chapter 6, Jesus gives his first sermon in Nazareth where both his family and neighbors reject him. Read 6:4. This is the man who amazes crowds with his teachings, heals disease, and exorcises demons. I can't imagine his family and neighbors rejecting him. In Acts, his brother James leads the Jesus movement in Jerusalem after the crucifixion, and his mother and siblings are members of that first congregation (Acts 1:14). As this obvious contradiction suggests, Mark 6:1–6 is a fictional story. Why invent it? The editor of the Gospel wants to make the point that even his family and neighbors don't get it. They are Jews. They do not understand the role Jesus will play in God's plan for salvation. God has given up on the Jews.

The disciples do not understand the meaning or the significance of the feeding of the five thousand and Jesus' walking on water. Why? Because God has closed their minds. Read Mark 6:52. There is a second feeding of the four thousand in chapter 8, and the disciples still don't get it. Jesus wonders if their minds are still closed. Can you believe God acts in this way? Can this be history? Do you want to believe in a God who closes peoples' minds in order to deny them salvation?

> Why are you talking about having no bread? Do you not yet understand? Have you no perception? Are your minds closed? Have you eyes that do not see, ears that do not hear? (Mark 8:17)

Mark's point to his congregation is that all of the Jews have rejected Jesus—even the disciples. The story makes little sense as history. The disciples had an intense relationship with Jesus. They all traveled together. They spent many nights together sleeping under the stars. As a result, there were many opportunities for them to ask questions concerning actions or teachings they did not understand.

In chapter 8, Jesus heals the blind man in two stages (8:22–26). After the first attempt, the man sees people as trees. So, Jesus tries again, and this time it works. Don't even go into the village, Jesus tells the man. Jews are forbidden from learning about the cure. This miracle story is only found in Mark. Mark uses it to make an important theological point, which will become clear in the next story.

At Caesarea Philippi (8:27–33), Jesus asks the disciples who the people think he is. He receives several answers. Peter eventually declares him to be the Messiah. Jesus sternly orders him to tell no one. Later he explains to the disciples that the Son of Man must undergo much suffering, be rejected by the elders, killed, and then rise up on the third day. Peter objects to this teaching. He doesn't like the idea of Jesus suffering. For him, the messiah is the traditional king sent by God to establish his kingdom on earth. Such kings don't suffer. He takes Jesus aside and rebukes him. In response, Jesus says, "Get behind me Satan" (8:33). Jesus will be a different kind of Messiah, the Son of Man who suffers. How does this relate to the miracle of the blind man? Peter sees only trees. He only has partial understanding.

At the transfiguration (9:2-11), Jesus takes Peter, James, and John up on the mountain with him. Several spectacular events take place. Toward the end of these events, a cloud appears—God often speaks in a cloud—from which God declares Jesus to be his Son. However, just prior to God speaking, the three disciples are overcome with fear, and the experience is over for them. They miss God speaking about Jesus as his Son (9:8). Why? They are Jews. Again, Matthew softens this point by allowing the three disciples to hear God's voice, an editorial change I will explain in more detail in the next chapter.

Following the transfiguration, Jesus teaches the disciples in private about the Son of Man who must be betrayed, killed, and then will rise up in three days. The disciples don't get it (9:30-32). James and John don't get it when they ask Jesus for a special place in the kingdom. Jesus scolds them (10:35-38). These two disciples see him as a royal Messiah, the most prevalent expectation. They want cabinet positions in the new Israel ruled by Jesus.

When Jesus is arrested, the disciples flee. They have been instructed about what it means to follow Jesus, and they can't live up to the requirements. Peter will deny Jesus three times. This rejection theme is repeated again and again and again.

There is a surprise ending to Mark's Gospel, and it is shocking (16:1-8). This is always a good strategy when telling a story. Three women go to the tomb to anoint Jesus' body. While there, a young man tells them that Jesus has risen and will meet the disciples in Galilee. He tells the women to report the good news to the disciples. What is interesting is that the women don't follow these instructions because they become afraid. The implication is that the disciples never hear about the resurrected Jesus. The fear problem again. This is fiction. The women include Jesus' mother. The news is joyous. The reaction of the women makes no sense. You would think they would run to the disciples with this glorious news. But Mark wants to drive home the point that the disciples don't get it. God has deserted all Jews as a nation.

> "But you must go and tell his disciples and Peter, he is going before you to Galilee; it is there you will see him, just as he told you." And the woman came out and ran away from the tomb because they were frightened out of their wits; and they said nothing to a soul, for they were afraid. (Mark 16:7-8)

The climax to the story comes on the cross (15:39). As Jesus suffers on the cross and dies, the Roman centurion proclaims him to be the Son of God. The centurion is the first human in the story to make that declaration, and he is a gentile. This is the signal that God has changed his allegiance to the gentiles.

> The centurion, who was standing in front of him, had seen how he had died, and he said, "In truth this man was a son of God." (Mark 15:39)

Many Christians have misinterpreted this key passage. Jesus doesn't suffer on the cross as a sacrifice for our sins, but rather his suffering tells us something important about the divine/human relationship.

As Jesus dies on the cross, the veil at the temple is torn in two (15:38). This veil protected the hiddenness of God in the holy of holies, a small room in the temple where God was presumed to reside. The only person allowed in that room was the high priest and only once a year during the Yom Kippur celebration. The fact that the veil at the temple has been torn following Jesus' death signifies that access to God is now available to all those who believe in Jesus. It is no longer a monopoly of the high priest. To reflect on the suffering of Jesus makes God available to you in a real sense.

The parable of the owner of the vineyard summarizes Mark's story (12:1-12). In the story, a man plants a vineyard, rents it to tenants, and then goes abroad. He sends a servant to collect the rent, but the tenants refuse to pay. The servant is beaten and treated badly. The owner then sends several servants to collect his rent, who are killed. Finally, he sends his Son, who is also killed. The tenants are now convinced they will inherit the field. Instead, the owner returns, kills the tenants, and gives the field to others.

A vineyard is a common symbol for Israel. The owner of the vineyard is God; the tenants are Jews. The story tells us that while God chose the Jews, when the Messiah came they rejected him. As a result, God has rejected the Jews and has gone elsewhere. The fact that God sends his Son, specifically designated in uppercase, tells us the story comes from the early church. The Son is a title used by the early church to explain the significance of Jesus. Jesus never made that claim for himself, nor were people living at the time of his life making such claims about him. The editor of Mark's Gospel created this parable to pull together and dramatize his story of God rejecting the Jews.

To summarize the storyteller's presentation, Jesus is declared to be God's Son in the opening sentence of the Gospel, privately at his baptism, at the transfiguration where it is not heard, and by demons; but no human beings describe him this way or understand him to be God's Son until the centurion makes that declaration at his death. The centurion was a gentile. Because the Jews as a nation have rejected Jesus, God has moved over to the gentiles.

This is good story telling, amazingly creative in its inception. The listeners can hear and sense the answer to their question about their new status as God's people. The one thing Mark's story is not is history. The story most likely comes from a gifted storyteller. It was almost certainly performed several times before it was written down some time after 70 CE.

Scriptural texts in the ancient world consisted of a string of letters with no separation between words or punctuation, which made them difficult to read. The typical scroll was also several feet long, which made it awkward to handle. They were also expensive, especially for the small Galilean villages where Jesus' ministry was focused. A scroll was also awkward to hold and read. For these reasons an official storyteller was often connected to a synagogue or a temple.

These storytellers did not read sacred texts, they performed. Such a performance was not a mechanical recital but a creative act. Performers played on audience emotions. They changed facts, exaggerated, and focused on the dramatic. No performer wants to appear boring. Each performance was different, even when given by the same performer. The idea of an original version of a story that was written down makes no sense. Eventually a scribe put one of the performances into writing.[6] This process of Gospel creation makes it hard to believe that Mark's Gospel could in any way reflect the literal word of God of conservative Christian belief.

To change the subject somewhat, the story of God's rejection of the Jews may explain the puzzle presented by the eleven verses added to Mark (16:8–20) by a scribe, which I mentioned briefly in the previous section. These eleven verses contain a poorly written summary of the resurrection stories presented in the other three Gospels. Ninety-five percent of New Testament scholars take this position.[7] My Bible, *The Jerusalem Bible*, was put together by the Roman Catholic Church. In a footnote, the editors agree with this judgment. The only Christians who believe these verses represent the literal word of God are those unfortunate ones who pick up snakes in their hands and believe they won't be harmed from drinking deadly poison. (See Mark 16:17–18.)

Scholars offer two possible solutions to this puzzle. The first is that the Gospel does in fact end at 16:8, and the second theory is that the last page of an earlier manuscript was lost, which contained a resurrection story. If the Gospel does end at 16:8, this does not deny the resurrection, but it suggests that the disciples didn't participate in it. This suggestion fits the Jewish rejection story nicely, which is why I prefer it as the best solution to the puzzle posed by the added text.

6. Dewey, *Oral Ethos of the Early Church*.
7. Black, *Perspectives on the Ending of Mark*.

The Gospel of Mark

CONFLICT STORIES

The conflicts between Jesus and the scribes and Pharisees are well documented in each of the four Gospels. Mark's Gospel contains several such encounters. That the stories in Mark are fictional accounts is apparent. To begin with, both groups were based in Jerusalem. (See Mark 3:22 and 7:1–23.) There is no evidence that either group ever traveled to the tiny villages of rural Galilee. Such travel involved a five-day walk. It is also important to remember that Jesus was a peasant teacher in an age with primitive communications. It is very unlikely that his message became known in Jerusalem. Some form of this conflict is possible in John's three-year organization scheme where Jesus makes several trips to Jerusalem, but the conflicts between the scribes and Pharisees reported in Mark's Gospel are very unlikely to have taken place.

The real venom expressed in Mark's stories also make it unlikely the disputes took place during Jesus' ministry. While the Pharisees would have disapproved of his eating with sinners, his not caring whether the disciples washed their hands before eating, and his healing on the Sabbath, these differences would not be enough to have them plot his destruction. (See Mark 3:6 and Matt 12:14.) Differences between Jewish sects in the first century were well accepted.[8] This venom suggests the real issues were about who would control the synagogue after the Great War, the Pharisees or the followers of Jesus.

Again, it is important to remember that fictional stories in ancient biographies were created to express important truths about the subject under study. In this case, the conflict stories were used as a foil to contrast the religion of Jesus with the Jewish establishment. In 2:6–9, the editor of Mark includes a story of who can forgive sins. According to Jewish belief, only God could forgive sins. The editor of Mark uses the story to declare that the Son of Man also has the power to forgive sins (2:10).

---

8. See Vermes, *Jesus the Jew*.

THE PASSION NARRATIVE

Mark is believed to be the primary author of the passion narrative for the Synoptic Gospels. The story is found in chapters 14 and 15 of his Gospel. The story begins with a woman anointing Jesus with a precious oil in Bethany (14:3). It is followed by Judas's betrayal (14:10–11), the Last Supper (14:18–26), and Jesus' prayer at Gethsemane to be relieved from his burden to fulfill God's plan (14:32–36). Jesus is then arrested (14:43–52), is tried before the Sanhedrin (14:53–64), and has a hearing before Pilate (15:1–5). At the conclusion of the hearing, Pilate offers to free Jesus, but the crowd chooses to free Barabbas instead (15:6–15). Jesus is then placed on a cross to die (15:16–38). The story ends with his burial (15:43–46).[9]

It is important to note that there are few, if any, eyewitnesses at these events. There were no witnesses at the Gethsemane scene where Jesus prays alone or followers of Jesus at his two trials. It should not be surprising, therefore, that there are some significant historical problems with Mark's story.

The first is the trial before the Sanhedrin. The Sanhedrin functioned as both court and legislature in first-century Palestine. It was the highest ruling body in Jewish colonial Palestine. Such a trial, as described in the Synoptics, was forbidden by Jewish law to take place during the Passover festival. Jewish law also forbade such trials at night; and, for a death sentence to be issued, the Sanhedrin had to consider the case twice. All these rules were violated in Mark's story. Josephus, the first-century Jewish historian, reports hundreds of crucifixions under Pilate without a trial. The question is why Jesus would be treated differently. To the Romans, he was a Galilean peasant who was seen as a troublemaker. Galilee was famous for its troublemakers. The most efficient way to deal with such threats was to arrest the troublemaker and place him on a cross in killing fields that were permanent fixtures. Roman colonial rule did not require a trial as a matter of criminal justice.

---

9. Over the years I have consulted several sources regarding the passion narrative. The most helpful ones include Borg and Crossan, *Last Week*; Crossan, *Birth of Christianity*; Brown, *Death of the Messiah*; Ehrman, *Jesus*; Theissen, *Sociology of Early Palestinian Christianity*; and Vermes, *Jesus the Jew*.

The Gospel of Mark

A trial in the supercharged atmosphere in Jerusalem at Passover would have been dangerous. When looked at in terms of the evidence presented above, I do not believe a trial took place.

Another major historical problem is the burial of Jesus. Such burials following a crucifixion were against Roman policy. No one crucified was buried.[10] Instead, victims were left on the cross for animals to devour them. The point was to make the spectacle so horrifying that political troublemakers would be deterred from challenging Roman rule. Again, believers who claim the burial of Jesus took place must explain why Jesus was an exception to this policy.

Then there is the picture of Pilate in the Gospel stories. First, the precedent to free one prisoner at Passover (the Barabbas story) is fiction. It had never been done before Jesus' crucifixion or in years following his crucifixion. Second, Pilate is viewed as a reasonable man, sympathetic toward Jesus, and seeing him as innocent. The problem here is that Pilate was not a reasonable man. Josephus portrays him as mean, petty, cruel, and ruthless. Ten years after the crucifixion Rome replaced him because of excessive cruelty.[11]

The role the crowd plays in the story is also suspect. Pilate pleads with the crowd to free Jesus. The question here is why Pilate would allow the crowd to play a role during Passover. It was a very dangerous time for Rome. Jerusalem grew from sixty thousand to three hundred thousand people during this time. These Jews hated Rome. To engage the crowd was to play with fire. Pilate may not have been a reasonable man, but he wasn't stupid.

In addition, there are many less significant historical problems to consider. In Mark's story, the arrest, two trials, crucifixion, death, and burial take place within a twenty-four-hour period. Crucifixions often required three days for the victim to succumb to death. The time frame presented in the Gospels is not credible.

---

10. See Crossan and Reed, *Excavating Jesus*, 245–46.
11. For a good discussion of the passion narrative as a fictional account, see Crossan, *Historical Jesus*, 354–94. For specifics relating to the trial and role of Pilate, see 390–91.

When Jesus dies, there is an eclipse of the sun that lasts for three hours (15:33). You don't have to be an astronomer to know that eclipses don't last that long. The question then becomes, Why did Mark include the eclipse in his story? The answer is quite apparent: because Amos prophesied it (Amos 8:19). This is a good example of prophecy creating history.

The story where Judas betrays Jesus is also suspect. While it is probable that Judas did betray Jesus, it most likely didn't occur in the way Mark describes it. According to Mark's story, Judas was needed to identify Jesus for the Jewish authorities, but in fact he was well known to them. He had taught in the temple for almost a week prior to his arrest. It is more probable that Judas convinced Pilate that Jesus wanted to be king, a real threat to Roman control of Palestine that had to be dealt with.

Finally, there is a problem with the role the crowd played in convicting Jesus. Mark describes enthusiastic crowds accompanying Jesus on his entry into Jerusalem (11:8–10). Why did they change their tune as the Barabbas story suggests?

While there may have been historical memory in creating Mark's story like the betrayal by Judas, the story is primarily a work of fiction. The question now becomes why such a story was invented. The problem for the followers of Jesus was to explain how Jesus could be the Messiah. He was not a king or a military leader. In the minds of first-century Jews, God would never have allowed such a person to die on a cross. Eventually these followers began to see Jesus in terms of the suffering servant portrayed in Isaiah. Isaiah describes a righteous man who dies in obedience to God and as an offering to others. In this latter sense, he was a man who bears our grief and carries our sorrow (Isa 53:4). He is a man who is powerful precisely because he is without power—a gentle, humble, good man.

A good example of this picture is found in Mark's presentation of Jesus' trial before the Sanhedrin (14:60–65). When the chief priest asks Jesus if he is the Messiah, the Son of God, Jesus refuses to answer the question directly. "The words are your own," Jesus answered. The chief priest proceeds to tear his clothes, and he accuses Jesus of blasphemy. Jesus remains silent in face of these charges, reminiscent of the suffering servant who remained silent as he was led to his slaughter (Isa 53:7). Members of the Sanhedrin respond by spitting in his face. This recalls the physical abuse endured by the suffering servant.

> For my part, I made no resistance neither did I turn away. I offered my back to those who struck me, my cheeks to those who tore at my beard; I did not cover my face against insult and spittle. (Isa 50:6)

Lacking historical evidence on what transpired when Jesus was crucified, a story emerged to explain these events. The story was created for oral presentation and was probably performed several times before attaining written form. While we have no clues as to who the original storyteller was, we do have a good idea as to why he created the story. The storyteller invented the story to explain to Mark's gentile community that Jesus was a messiah who was destined to suffer. This is a good example of how fiction was used in the writing of ancient biographies. Storytellers invented their stories to make an important point about the subject of their study that they believed was absolutely true about him.

CONCLUSION

This concludes our presentation of Mark's Gospel. I have included in the analysis the most significant elements of the Gospel with two exceptions. The first is Mark's resurrection story (16: 9–20), which I deal with in chapter 5. The second exception was Mark's nine miracle stories. These stories most likely came to the final editor in a written collection from which he chose his favorites. As we will see when we discuss the miracle stories at length in chapter 5, the stories in Mark were fictional accounts.

As is evident from the analysis throughout this chapter, the Gospel of Mark was not written by an evangelist who was an eyewitness to the events of Jesus' life. Instead, the elements of the Gospel emerged over a period of years most likely culminating with the rejection story around 70 CE or somewhat later. An editor put all the parts together—the story of the coming of God's kingdom, the rejection story, the miracle stories, the conflict stories involving the scribes and Pharisees, and the passion narrative. The editor invented the one-year ministry with a final week in Jerusalem as well as the transition devices linking the elements of the Gospel together. It was an impressive achievement. A leader within the early church most likely added the Son of Man statements, and a scribe added the eleven verses describing the resurrection at the end of the Gospel. The written Gospel we have emerged toward the end of the second century and was based on a collaborative effort containing the several parts we have described in this chapter. When you add it up—three storytellers, a final editor, church leaders, and two or more scribal entries—you get the idea that the writing of the Gospel of Mark was a committee effort.

3

The Gospel of Matthew

GOSPEL MECHANICS

THE GOSPEL OF MATTHEW is the story of the Jewish Messiah who fulfills all of God's promises and Jewish hopes. Jesus is portrayed as the son of David sent to the house of Israel (Matt 10:5-5 and 15:24). Matthew embraces Jewish law. One is saved by obedience to it. As such it is a Gospel about morals and ethics. The teachings of Jesus play a prominent role. Traditionally it has been the favorite of Christians because of its inclusion of the virgin birth story and the Sermon on the Mount.

The date of writing is set at 85–90 CE. The Gospel clearly relies on a written version of Mark so it must be later. Matthew uses 90 percent of Mark. It is easier to explain that Matthew followed Mark than to explain why Mark would have ignored 50 percent of Matthew. It also reflects the conflict for control of Judaism that was raging between Jewish Christians and the Pharisees following the destruction of Jerusalem in 70 CE.

The Pharisees gained the dominant position within the Jewish diaspora throughout the Hellenistic world, and they demanded correct belief. In this regard, they did not accept Jesus as the Messiah, which posed a threat to Jewish Christians remaining in the synagogue. They began expelling followers of Jesus in the 80s.

Most scholars view Matthew as representing a community that had recently separated from the synagogue and was looking for a way to maintain their Jewish identity. In several places you see the final editor referring to "their synagogue" or "your synagogue." See Matt 4:23, 9:35, 12:9, 13:54, and 23:34. And yet it is clear that Jesus' message was to the lost sheep of Israel (Matt 15:24).

This conflict for control of Judaism after the destruction of Jerusalem in 70 CE is an interesting one. As was noted in the last chapter, most New Testament scholars argue that at the time of Jesus the Pharisees were a small party confined to Jerusalem. There is no historical evidence of Pharisees operating in the tiny rural villages of Galilee at the time of Jesus. Despite these historical facts, Matthew presents the conflict in Galilee, which suggests the stories were largely invented.

Scholars explain this bitter conflict in an interesting way. It was a consequence of the Jewish/Roman War. Prior to 70 CE, the Jewish religion was centered in the temple. When the temple was destroyed in 70 CE, the central focus of the Jewish faith shifted to the synagogue where the Pharisees played the leading role. After 70 CE, the Pharisees became the dominant force in Judaism.

Both the Pharisees and the followers of Jesus reestablished themselves in the Hellenistic world after the Great War. The two groups fought each other in the synagogue over the future of Judaism. The conflict was often bitter. The writers of the Gospels created stories that reset this conflict forty years earlier in rural Galilee with Jesus as one of the chief protagonists. In this way, the editors of the Gospels were able to define the religion of Jesus by contrasting his teachings with the religion of the Pharisees.

Returning to our discussion of Gospel mechanics in Matthew, we have no idea who wrote the Gospel. It was common practice in the ancient world to name a work after a person whose name would enhance the work's credibility. Moses was named as the author of the first five books of the Old Testament, Solomon was named as the author of the Book of Wisdom, Proverbs, and the Song of Songs, and David was named as the author of many of the Psalms. I have already argued against the idea that any of the

Gospels were written by an eyewitness. It is also important to note that the earliest texts we have of the Gospels were not named. Names of authors were added to the Gospels toward the end of the second century to differentiate between the them. As a result, the idea of the disciple Matthew writing this Gospel is not credible. His name was attached to the Gospel to honor a disciple and to enhance the Gospel's believability.

There is some evidence, however, about the place of writing. Scholars select Syria as the best choice. There was a large Jewish community in Antioch in the first century, and Matthew states in 4:24 that Jesus' reputation spread rapidly throughout Syria. That's not overwhelming evidence, but it is all we have.

The Gospel contains three main sources. The first source was Mark. Ninety percent of the material in Mark is found in Matthew. It is clear that whoever created Matthew copied Mark. Plagiarism was obviously not a problem in the first century. This material represents 50 percent of Matthew's Gospel. Twenty-five percent of the Gospel comes from Matthew's own sources, sources designated M, which remain a mystery. The remaining 25 percent comes from Q.

Q denotes the German word *Quelle*, which means "source." Johannes Weiss first proposed the idea of Q more than one hundred years ago. Q is a mystery source that has never been found—most probably a casualty of the Great War (66–73). There are passages in Matthew and Luke that are word for word the same. These passages are found nowhere else in the New Testament. The best explanation is Q, with each writer having a copy on his table.

Compare Matt 3:7–10 and Luke 3:7–9 cited below. This is a John the Baptist story only found in Matthew and Luke. After a different introduction in which Matthew has John speak to Pharisees and Sadducees and Luke to a crowd, it is word for word the same. Note how this Q story is used in the two Gospels. It is an insert that the final editors of the two Gospels use differently. Matthew concludes the story with the idea that Jesus is superior to John, while Luke goes in a totally different direction with some ethical teachings. Editors selected stories from collections like Q to meet the needs of their own agenda.

> But when he saw a number of Pharisees and Sadducees coming for baptism he said to them, "Brood of vipers, who warned you to fly from the retribution that is coming? But if you are repentant, produce the appropriate fruit, and do not presume to tell yourselves, 'We have Abraham for our father,' because I tell you, God can raise children for Abraham from these stones. Even now the ax is laid to the roots of the trees so that any tree which fails to produce good fruit will be cut down and thrown on the fire." (Matt 3:7–11)

> He said, therefore, to the crowds who came to be baptized by him, "Brood of vipers, who warned you to fly from the retribution that is coming? But if you are repentant, produce the appropriate fruit, and do not presume to tell yourselves, 'We have Abraham for our father,' because I tell you, God can raise children for Abraham from these stones. Even now the ax is laid to the roots of the trees so that any tree which fails to produce good fruit will be cut down and thrown on the fire." (Luke 3:7–9)

Q is a collection of Jesus sayings with an estimated 225 verses. Not all of the saying parallels are verbatim as was the case in the John the Baptist story cited above, but those not verbatim have similar wording and are only found in Matthew and Luke. Q has no birth story or passion narrative. The sayings are listed in a random order. Q is believed to be the earliest source of the Jesus tradition. The date for writing is estimated to be in the 50s. The fact that the stories within it have a very Palestinian flavor, and most scholars believe the stories were originally written in Aramaic, make it a very important source of the Jesus tradition. The collection some refer to as a Gospel has a strong eschatological flavor. Judgment is seen as imminent, with Jesus portrayed as the Son of Man, the bringer of that judgment.[1]

Recent scholarship has concluded that Q was established in two stages. In stage one, Jesus is pictured as a teacher of wisdom and a prophet called by God to announce the imminent coming of his kingdom to Israel. Stage two adds material about the Son of

---

1. See Edwards, *Theology of Q*; and Casey, *Aramaic Approach to Q*.

Man who comes from the clouds of heaven to bring judgment and to rescue the righteous and take them to heaven.[2]

As I will point out in the section on the teachings of Jesus that follows, these Son of Man statements came from the early church. What is interesting about the statements is that, with two exceptions, they all come from the mouth of Jesus in the first person. There were many self-proclaimed Christian prophets running around Palestine in the first century who claimed they spoke for Jesus. They were more than comfortable putting words in Jesus' mouth. They claimed this right because they were filled with the spirit of Jesus.[3]

One last comment on Q: please remember all of the above is speculation. Q has never been found. Some scholars argue it doesn't exist, that the parallel passages are explained by Luke copying from Matthew, although this is a minority position.

The Gospel of Matthew is organized around five major collections of Jesus' teachings called discourses. All five start with a similar introduction and end with the words: "And Jesus came to the end of these sayings." These discourses include the Sermon on the Mount (5:1—7:28), missionary teachings of Jesus (10:1—11:1), parables (13:1–52), teachings on church life (18:1–35), and teachings regarding the final judgment (24:1–44). With this arrangement we see how the oral tradition affected the writing of the Gospel. The Gospel is organized around collections of like stories rather than chronology. A detailed discussion of the five discourses follows in this chapter while a further discussion of the oral tradition occurs in the next chapter on Luke.

THE NEW MOSES

While all the Synoptic Gospels reflect the view of the early church that Jesus became the Son of Man after the resurrection, they differ as to the role Jesus played in history. It was Matthew's view that

---

2. Koester, *Ancient Christian Gospels*, 128–70.
3. Casey, *Aramaic Approach to Q*.

Jesus was the new Moses—a popular expectation for the coming Messiah at the time. Matthew shapes much of his Gospel to make this point.[4] Here is what he says.

The virgin birth story (1:11—4:11) is unique to Matthew.[5] When a story is unique to a Gospel, you need to pay close attention to it because it signals an important theme. In this case, the storyteller is telling his listeners Jesus is the new Moses.

Matthew's virgin birth story is patterned after the birth of Moses in Exod 1:15—2:10. Herod plays the same role as the Egyptian pharaoh. Both are tyrants threatened by the birth of a rival to their thrones. In the two stories, an infant is saved from the evil king bent on destroying him. Babies are killed (Exod 1:22 and Matt 2:16). The child must flee for his life and return home only after the evil king has died. The ending for the all-clear signal is expressed word for word the same: "and those seeking your life are dead." Compare Exod 4:19 and Matt 2:21, and note another example of the use of the Old Testament in Gospel story creation.

To digress briefly, Matthew's virgin birth story changes Mark's focus on Jesus as the Son of God to a portrayal of Jesus as the Son of David, a descendant of Abraham. (Compare Matt 1:1 with Mark 1:1.) Matthew has six references to Jesus as the Son of David in his Gospel. This change is an example of one of the great confusions in the New Testament. How is salvation achieved? There are four models that float randomly throughout the four Gospels. The first is the traditional messiah idea where God would send a king in the image of David to rescue Israel, the view expressed in Matt 1:1. Then there is the idea that God would establish a kingdom in Israel, which he alone would rule. This is the position of Jesus, which we will examine later on in this chapter. Finally, there is the activity of the Son of Man. There are two views of how he will bring in salvation. There are some passages that suggest he will return

---

4. The story in Matthew of Jesus as the new Moses is well established within the scholarly literature. See Ehrman, *New Testament*, 82–90; Burridge, *Four Gospels*, 72–74; and Carter, *What Are They Saying About Matthew?*

5. The virgin birth story in Matthew is a work of fiction, a point I will make clear in the next chapter when I compare it to Luke's virgin birth story.

from the clouds of heaven as judge with the righteous establishing a kingdom on earth and those who are evil being punished. There are other passages indicating he will return to rescue the righteous and take them to heaven.

Returning to Matthew's discussion of Jesus as the new Moses, he patterns his temptation story (4:1–11) after Moses's farewell address to Israel. See Deut 8:1–6. In his speech, Moses reminds the people of their forty years of testing in the wilderness. Jesus was tested in the wilderness for forty days. While in the wilderness, the devil tested both Jesus and the people under Moses with hunger. In responding to the devil (Matt 4:4), Jesus quotes word for word God's response to Moses (Deut 8:3).

The Sermon on the Mount (5:1—7:29) is also unique to Matthew. The event takes place on a mountain. Moses receives the law on a mountain while Jesus reforms the law on one. More telling are Jesus' words when reforming that law. There are several "You have learned how it was said to our ancestors." Jesus then cites a law given to Moses. He ends with the words "But I say to you." Jesus concludes by defining the new meaning for the law. The reference to Moses couldn't be clearer. It is also clear that as the new Moses Jesus was claiming to be the final interpreter of Jewish law.

There are several features of the transfiguration story (17:1–8) that recall Moses at Sinai. A selected group of companions go up on a mountain. A cloud encases them, which leads to a revelation of God's glory. Read Exod 24:9–18. Then Matthew adds a phrase to Mark's story: "his face shone like the sun" (17:2). Read Exod 34:29–35. This is the story where Moses comes down from the mountain after receiving the Ten Commandments. The skin on his face "shone like the sun." First-century Jews would not miss this reference to Moses.

When Jesus meets his disciples on a mountain in Galilee for their resurrection encounter, his final instructions include the clause "and teach them to observe all the commandments I gave you." This is part of Matthew's important theme that believers are saved by doing good works and obeying the law. These words are unique to Matthew and again invoke Moses's farewell address to Israel in Deuteronomy.

> All the commandments I enjoin on you today you must keep and observe so that you may live and increase in numbers and enter into the land that Yahweh promised on oath to your fathers. (Deut 8:1)

The editor of Matthew organized the Gospel in such a way as to remind Jews of Moses. What did Moses do? He saved the people of God and created a new religion. That's exactly what Jesus will do. This story is most likely the work of a gifted storyteller whose story, after several presentations, became part of the written oral tradition. The editor of Matthew was then able to select it and make changes and additions that suited his purpose and were required to fit seamlessly in his Gospel.

THE VOICE OF THE EDITOR

You see the voice of the editor in the creation of the new Moses story discussed above. You can also see the editor of Matthew's voice in the fascinating and subtle changes he makes in Mark's story of God's rejection of the Jews. No Jews are allowed in Mark's story to learn that Jesus is the Son of God. The editor of Matthew does not feel so strongly about God's rejection of the Jews, and so he softens Mark's story in several places. He also had a higher view of the disciples than Mark.

I have already shown the subtle change he made in the story of Jesus' baptism where God spoke from heaven to Jesus, declaring him to be the Son of God in a way that enabled all the Jews present with John the Baptist to hear (Matt 3:17). In Mark's story of the transfiguration (Mark 9:2–11), God declares Jesus to be his Son. However, just prior to God speaking, the three disciples present are overcome with fear, which prevents them from hearing God's declaration. In Matthew's version of the story (17:5–6), the exact same words are used but God speaks first, before the three disciples are overcome with fear, which enables them to hear God's declaration of Jesus as his Son. The editor of Matthew does nothing more than change the sentence order.

Following the transfiguration story in Mark, Jesus teaches his disciples in private about the role the Son of Man will play in Israel's salvation. The disciples can't picture Jesus as a salvation figure who must be betrayed, killed, and then rise up to heaven in three days before returning to earth to rescue the righteous (Mark 9:30–32). James and John demonstrate this lack of understanding by asking for cabinet positions in the new Israel ruled by Jesus. They see Jesus as a royal Messiah, a king, which was the most widely held messianic expectation among Jews at that time. For their lack of understanding, Jesus scolds them (Mark 10:35–38). Matthew softens this story by having the mother of James and John make the request on behalf of her sons (20:20–23). Matthew has a higher view of the disciples than Mark and is not so obsessed with making the point that all the Jews including the disciples rejected Jesus.

The voice of the editor is not the only voice that floats through the four Gospels. As the next section will demonstrate, Jesus' voice is also in evidence. Finally, as the next section will also demonstrate, there is the distinctive voice of the first-century church. Because the four Gospels don't come in the form of a play with each voice labeled, differentiating among the different voices can be a challenge.

THE VOICE OF JESUS

The voice of Jesus is most clearly expressed in his teachings regarding the kingdom of God. What the historical Jesus proclaimed was the coming of God's kingdom to the nation of Israel.

> Then he proclaimed the Good News from God. "The time has come," he said, "and the kingdom of God is close at hand. Repent, and believe the Good News." (Mark 1:14–15; see also Mark 9:1 and Matt 9:35)

The Lord's Prayer contains words from Jesus that scholars believe are most likely to be authentic. Where is God's kingdom?

> So you should pray like this: "Our Father in heaven, may your name be held holy, your kingdom come, your will be done on earth as in heaven." (Matt 6:10)

Jesus prays for God's kingdom to come and for his will to be done on earth as it is in heaven. Heaven is the model, but the kingdom is on earth. Jesus promises his disciples they will sit on twelve thrones in Israel, the idea being that each disciple will preside over a Jewish tribe.

> You are the men who have stood by me faithfully in my trials; and now I will confer a kingdom on you, just as my Father conferred one on me: you will eat and drink at my table in my kingdom, and you will sit on thrones to judge the twelve tribes of Israel. (Luke 22:20-21; see also Matt 19:28)

When the Pharisees ask Jesus when the kingdom will come, Jesus responds, "The kingdom of God is among you" (Luke 17:20-21). This statement again indicates the kingdom is on earth. The kingdom of God refers not to a place primarily, but to a situation in which God rules, as the Luke passage cited above suggests. It is about a new way of living and relating to people, a kingdom where the power of love would replace the power of evil. What such a place is like is defined in the parables.[6] As Jesus says over and over again in the Synoptic Gospels (Matthew, Mark, and Luke), these parables reveal the mysteries of the kingdom of God.

The kingdom of God is like a treasure a man finds in a field—a whole new world opens up (Matt 13:44-45). As the parables of the lost sheep and the prodigal son tell us, the kingdom of God is like finding something precious that was lost. What is the kingdom of God like, Jesus asks in Luke 13:18-19? It's like a mustard seed—a feeling of love exploding inside you. The parable about the Pharisee and the tax collector tells us the kingdom of God will bring about a reversal of values (Luke 18:1-8). Several of Jesus' best loved parables contain this message: a Samaritan rescues a

---

6. For an informative discussion of Jesus' parables, see Levine, *Short Stories by Jesus*; and Jeremias, *Parables of Jesus*.

Jew (Luke 10:29-37), a landowner pays his day laborers the same for those who worked an eight-hour day as for those who worked a one-hour day (Matt 20:1-16), the wayward son is given a warm welcome home (Luke 15:11-32), enemies are forgiven, the last shall be first. As the parable of the sower tells us, God's rule will not take place by political means or military intervention, but by the peaceful spreading of God's word (Matt 13:23).

It is important to note that, in defining this kingdom, the parables are down to earth, the images based on Palestinian life. They are about vineyards, fig trees, weddings, tax collectors, children playing in the marketplace. No parable mentions the end of the world or the final judgment. This is a kingdom on earth for the people of Israel. As Jesus instructs his disciples:

> Do not make your way to Gentile territory, and do not enter any Samaritan town. Go instead to the lost sheep of the House of Israel; and as you go, proclaim that the kingdom of heaven is close at hand. (Matt 10:6-7)

The current state of affairs on earth was ruled by Satan. People in Palestine who were sick or demon possessed were seen as having bodies that had been taken over by Satan. What was Jesus doing about this situation? He was healing the sick and exorcising demons. Read Luke 11:20-21 and Matt 12:28. The battle for control of the earth had begun, and Jesus was winning. He was defeating Satan in order to create God's kingdom on earth.

The voice of the church was analyzed in the last chapter. To review briefly, we must first deal with the title Son of Man. There are many titles for Jesus that appear in the Gospels—Son of God, Son of David, Lord, prophet, teacher, rabbi, Son of Man. Son of Man is by far the most frequently used title. It appears eighty-one times in the Gospels. In all but two of these cases (Mark 8:38 and Luke 12:8), Jesus speaks as the Son of Man in the first person. It is the only title Jesus claims for himself. As I will point out below, these statements where Jesus speaks as the Son of Man in the first person were added to the Gospel by the early church. There are no confessional statements by followers of Jesus during his lifetime making this claim.

The church in the first century saw the resurrected Jesus as the Son of Man. It took some time for the followers of Jesus to come to this understanding. While these followers had a keen sense that Jesus was alive in some way, there was no idea in Judaism that the messiah would suffer. Deuteronomy 21:23 soundly proclaimed that anyone who hangs from a tree is cursed. In addition, after the Roman invasion in 70 CE, there was no Israel for God to establish his kingdom.

Because the close followers of Jesus had a strong sense that he was alive in some way and when no political restoration was achieved, the church latched on to the Son of Man idea. As I pointed out in the last chapter, the Son of Man myth was first expressed by the prophet Daniel. This figure is a preexistent, heavenly being who as God's divine agent would judge the world.

In most instances in the New Testament, this divine being comes from the clouds of heaven, but he is also understood to come from the depths of the ocean. The early church in Palestine interprets the resurrected Jesus in these terms. Stephen, the first Christian martyr, has a vision of Jesus in heaven at the right hand of God. Stephen proclaims him to be the Son of Man. Paul, though avoiding the title Son of Man, has a similar vision of Jesus in heaven. (See Acts 9:1–9.)

> But Stephen, filled with the Holy Spirit, gazed into heaven and saw the glory of God, and Jesus standing at God's right hand. "I can see heaven open," he said, and the Son of Man standing at the right hand of God. (Acts 7:55–57)

As time passed and the Jesus movement relocated in the Hellenistic world after 70 CE, the idea developed that salvation would no longer be given to the nation of Israel, which had ceased to exist, but rather to a small group of individuals in heaven. The Son of Man would swoop down to gather up this elect group of Jesus' followers to take them there. See Matt 24:30–31 and Mark 13:26.

The historical Jesus preaches about a kingdom coming in the near future, not about his own return. It is a kingdom for the Jewish nation within history. The Son of Man speaks about a kingdom in heaven, which is beyond history. History as we know it will end. The historical Jesus talks about saving a nation. The Son of Man talks about saving individuals in heaven. The message of Jesus is delivered from a human person on earth. The message of the Son of Man comes from a preexistent, divine being hidden in the presence of God until he emerges at the end of time from the clouds of heaven.

As Norman Perrin points out in his fascinating book *Rediscovering the Teachings of Jesus*, the same person could not be making both of these claims.[7] They are different voices. The Son of Man is the agent of the apocalypse, the judge that brings the end of history, and rescues the righteous taking them to heaven. The Jesus of the parables who announces the coming of God's kingdom describes what it would be like to live in such a place on earth. It is also significant that the title Son of Man is never used in a confessional way. There is no evidence that during his lifetime people thought of Jesus in this way. The church came to see Jesus as the Son of Man after the resurrection. To foster belief in Jesus as the Son of Man, Gospel writers from the early church put words in Jesus' mouth and placed those words in their Gospels. Son of Man statements are most often on the lips of Jesus. The early church has taken great liberties with these statements by putting words in Jesus' mouth.

To review, Matthew's Gospel includes four different views of what salvation is all about. The editor expresses at the outset the most prevalent view of a messiah returning as a king from the house of David to rescue Israel from her enemies. Then there is the view of Jesus that God, not the expected messiah, will bring his kingdom to the land of Israel, a kingdom where God will rule. Finally, there are two views regarding the Son of Man. One has him returning to Israel from heaven to establish a kingdom on earth (Matt 19:28–29). Matthew also has him returning to earth to take the elect to heaven (13:40–43 and 24:30–31).

---

7. Perrin, *Rediscovering the Teachings of Jesus*. This is a widely held view among New Testament scholars. See also Bultmann, *Jesus Christ and Mythology*; Fredriksen, *Jesus of Nazareth*; Allen, *Human Christ*; Vermes, *Authentic Gospel of Jesus*; and Ehrman, *Did Jesus Exist?*

JESUS FULFILLS SCRIPTURE

As I pointed out in the introduction, the Old Testament was a major source of story creation. The Jews did not view their sacred scripture as a history of the people of Israel, but rather as a blueprint of what God intended for the future. The Old Testament was predictive. It was seen as the word of God, which was addressed to the present as well as the past.

First-century Jewish Christians and many conservative Christians today believe Jesus fulfills Jewish scripture, that the writings in the Old Testament point to him. I was taught as a child that Jesus fulfilling scripture proves the historicity of the Christian Bible. In my book on Evangelical Christianity, I discredit this idea. I do it by testing several New Testament claims that Jesus fulfills scripture. It was a large research undertaking. I found there is little or no credibility to the idea. For a full discussion of my findings, you should consult my book.[8] For now, I will examine four fulfillment claims in Matthew. The first two come from the virgin birth story.

The final editor of Matthew more than any other of the Gospel writers made claims that Old Testament passages pointed directly to Jesus. Our first example comes from Matt 2:15. In the story, God tells Joseph in a dream to take the baby Jesus to Egypt in order to escape the wrath of Herod. Remember: Herod kills all those children in Matthew's virgin birth story. Matthew claims this action fulfills Hos 11:1, "I called my son out of Egypt." The Hosea passage refers to God's liberation of the people of Israel from their captivity in Egypt. Please explain to me how the great event of Israel's escape from Egypt as described in Exodus has any relation to God telling Joseph in a dream to take his family to Egypt to escape the wrath of Herod. Note too that the Hosea passage has God calling his son out of Egypt while Matthew's story has God call Joseph to Egypt.

The second example comes from Matt 2:18. When Herod kills all the children, Matthew claims this action fulfills Jer 31:15–16. A careful reading of the Jeremiah passage indicates a problem. The children Rachel laments in Jeremiah have not been killed, but

---

8. Herrick, *Case Against Evangelical Christianity*, 73–98.

rather they are lost. They are eventually found and returned. The two stories have few, if any, parallels.

As an aside while we are on the virgin birth story, the claim of Matthew and Luke that Jesus was born in Bethlehem is an example of prophecy creating history. Read Micah 5:2 where the prophet says the messiah would be born in Bethlehem. There is a large scholarly consensus that Jesus was in fact born in Nazareth. Because of the belief that the Old Testament is a blueprint of what God intends for the future, Matthew and Luke created their virgin birth stories to have Jesus born in Bethlehem. I suspect Matthew and Luke knew few, if any, historical details surrounding the birth of Jesus. However, God, through the prophet Micah, predicted the messiah would be born in Bethlehem. As a result, both Luke and Matthew invented stories to confirm Micah's prophecy. This point will become more convincing when you read a more detailed analysis of the two virgin birth stories in the next chapter.

The healing miracles are a rich source of prophecy fulfillment. One night the disciples bring to Jesus many people who are possessed by devils (Matt 8:16–17). Jesus casts out the evil spirits and cures the sick. According to Matthew's Gospel, these actions fulfill Isa 53:4. The Isaiah passage reads, "And yet ours were the sufferings he bore, ours the sorrows he carried." This reference to Isaiah is taken from the famous suffering servant passages. If you read the specific reference in Isaiah, you will discover the suffering servant does not cast out spirits and cure the sick. Instead, he bears their suffering and carries their sorrows. Jesus cures illness; the suffering servant feels pain. The author of Matthew is misleading here, or maybe a better word is careless.

Finally, in chapter 13 of Matthew, Jesus speaks to the people in parables. The implication is this is done so that the people will not understand. This fulfills the word of the prophet in Ps 78:2. (See 13:34–35.) To begin with, the reference Matthew has in mind is not taken from a prophet, but Ps 78. If you read the psalm in its entirety, you will note parables are used in the psalm to reveal meaning, not conceal it.

The writers of the Gospels were quick to indicate ways in which Jesus fulfilled scripture because it supported the idea that he was the Jewish Messiah. The four examples cited above, as well as the findings of the larger study in my book on Evangelical Christianity, suggest that their use of the Old Testament in this way was rather careless. Rather than prove the historicity of the Gospel record, it demonstrates that Gospel writing was a very human endeavor. Humans will go to incredible effort to lend support to beliefs they hold dearly.

MATTHEW'S DISCOURSES

Some scholars characterize Matthew's Gospel as Mark plus the discourses. Although this is a simplistic characterization, the five discourses are a significant addition. Each begins with an appropriate introduction pertaining to setting and ends with words indicating that Jesus was finished with what he had to say.[9]

The first one is Matthew's famous Sermon on the Mount (5:1—7:28). As I have explained before, the Sermon was a device created by the editor to gather together and present Jesus' teachings. Each of the discourses is presented in the same way. With regard to the Sermon on the Mount, it consists of a collection of Jesus' teachings that call for a radically new approach to living within society. Sixty-two of the 106 verses come from Q and are therefore similar to Luke's version (Luke 6:20–49).[10] The point of the teaching is that one must go beyond literal obedience to the law to the spirit behind it. A follower of Jesus lives not by the norms of society, but rather by the character of God.

> You have heard how it was said, you shall not commit adultery. But I say this to you, if a man looks at a woman lustfully, he has already committed adultery with her in his heart. (Matt 5:27)

---

9. Most scholarly treatments of Matthew deal with the discourses. One of the best I found comes in P. T. France's commentary, *Gospel of Matthew*.

10. See Carter, *What Are They Saying About Matthew's Sermon on the Mount?*, 12.

The second discourse deals with instructions given to the disciples (10:1—11:1). The discourse is presented as a speech by Jesus that consists of a series of related Jesus sayings that most likely came from a written collection of sayings in the oral tradition. The speech provides instructions for the disciples and points out some of the challenges they will face in carrying out their missionary work.

The third discourse is a collection of parables (13:1–53), which parallels Mark's collection in 4:1–34. The device the editor creates is a speech Jesus gives from a boat most likely in the Sea of Galilee, although the exact location is not given. The parables are about the workings of God's kingdom, which the crowds don't understand. Matthew disagrees with Mark in that the disciples do understand the teachings hidden within the parables (Matt 13:51). As I have pointed out several times, Matthew has a more positive view of the disciples than Mark.

The fourth discourse is on the church (18:1—19:1) and provides instructions on how to live within the community. Jesus answers two questions posed by his disciples that the discourse comprises. The first question is, Who is the greatest in the kingdom of heaven? Jesus answers that children are the greatest. Why? Because of their low position in society, which enables them to recognize their dependency. Several sayings follow that illustrate different aspects of Jesus' answer.

The second question relates to how one should deal with a sinning member of the community. The device in this case is a private meeting Jesus has with his disciples. The answer is to confront him gently with his transgression. If several such attempts fail to turn the transgressor around, that person must be asked to leave the community. Again, several illustrative sayings follow. Toward the end you find the famous teaching on forgiveness where Jesus tells Peter that he must forgive his brother seventy-seven times (18:21).

The last discourse deals with the end times and is found in chapters 24 and 25. The device here is a private meeting Jesus has with his disciples on the Mount of Olives. In chapter 24, Jesus predicts the coming destruction of the temple and answers the disciples' questions pertaining to when this event will occur.

He then answers the related eschatological question of when the Son of Man will arrive from the clouds of heaven. This part of the discourse is taken directly from Mark. (See chapter 13 in Mark.) Chapter 24 concludes with the parable of the conscientious steward, and chapter 25 contains three additional parables that illustrate Jesus' teachings on the end times. These four parables are Matthew's additions to Mark.

With regard to the central purpose of this book, it is evident that the editor of Matthew selected sayings, parables, and teachings from the oral tradition in creating these discourses. These sources most likely came from a written collection of similar items, i.e., sayings of Jesus, parables, or teachings. The discourses are fictional devices created by the editor to make important points regarding the teachings and ministry of Jesus.

CONCLUSION

Matthew's Gospel was created over several years as stories developed about Jesus, which the final editor was able to select from. The new Moses story was probably first performed in a synagogue by the resident storyteller several years before the final editor of the Gospel skillfully integrated it into the basic storyline provided by Mark. As I pointed out in the introductory chapter, Matthew creates his genealogy to defend the birth of Jesus (Matt 1:1–16). It seems possible that the final editor took the genealogy from the oral tradition and added four gentile women with discredited sexual pasts to make the point that something special can come from such a past.

The five discourses play a major role in the Gospel that the final editor creates by inventing a situation (a sermon on a mountain) and then filling in the situation from relevant items taken from written listings of the items from the oral tradition. Much of this material came from the mysterious source Q. The softening of Mark's Jewish rejection story indicates the final editor was a skilled writer. He also corrects Mark's mistakes relating to the operation of Jewish institutions. In bringing all these parts together, the final

The Gospel of Matthew

editor again displays his considerable skill. In the next chapter, we will find that the final editor of Luke possessed similar skills.

4

The Gospel of Luke

GOSPEL MECHANICS

I LOVE THE GOSPEL of Mark because of the storyteller's creative tale of why God rejected the Jews. I love Matthew because of the focus on the teachings of Jesus—teachings which have been the guideposts of my life. I love Luke for its optimism, joy, life is a banquet point of view. Jesus is pictured in Luke as merciful and kind.[1]

The author of Luke begins his Gospel with a Prologue (1:1–4) where the editor points out his information about Jesus comes from the oral tradition. In the Prologue, he dedicates the Gospel to Theophilus. Such a dedication was a common practice in ancient biography. The name Theophilus means "lover of God," which suggests the Gospel is written for Christian believers.

As with the other Gospels, there are no good theories as to who wrote Luke. There is an old theory Luke was a traveling companion of Paul. The problem with this theory is that Luke's attitude toward Jewish law and his view of the resurrection couldn't have been more different from Paul. For Luke, one is saved by obeying Jewish law, while Paul posits salvation as a free gift from God, an

---

1. For a good discussion of the Gospel mechanics pertaining to Luke, see Cadbury, *Making of Luke-Acts*; Powell, *What Are They Saying About Luke?*; and Juel, *Luke-Acts*.

act of divine grace. With regard to the resurrection, Luke presents a very physical encounter between Jesus and his disciples, while Paul argues in favor of a vision experience, a topic we will examine in detail toward the end of this chapter.

Many scholars speculate that the author of Luke was a Hellenistic Christian; and while it is clear God is pictured as reaching out to gentiles in both the Gospel and Acts, God has not given up on Jews. Thousands of Jews are seen as accepting the gospel in Acts. (See chapters 2, 3, and 4.) As a Hellenistic Christian, the author of Luke displays considerable ignorance of Palestinian geography and Jewish religious traditions.

The date for the writing of the Gospel is set by general consensus at 85-90 CE, again speculated on without good evidence. It was clearly written after Mark, which is the only real evidence we have regarding the date of writing.

The author of Luke uses the same mixture of sources as Matthew. Mark accounts for 35 percent of his Gospel, Q for 20 percent, and the remaining 45 percent comes from his own sources labeled by scholars as L. From his own sources are found most of Jesus' well-loved parables that tell us so much about who he was and what he taught about God's kingdom. In a general sense, Luke takes the order of events from Mark and adds a great deal of his own material to Mark's account. These add-ons, material unique to Luke, tell us a great deal about the author's intention and theology, a topic we will explore in further detail when we discuss Luke's picture of the historical Jesus as Israel's last prophet.

The final editor wrote in polished Greek, the best Greek stylist in the New Testament. This same polished Greek appears in Acts. There is a general consensus among New Testament scholars that the author of Luke also wrote Acts. In addition to language, there are remarkable parallels between the two works. Peter is portrayed in Acts as being just like Jesus. He teaches with authority, heals the sick, and even brings people back to life. Paul is also viewed as the mirror image of Jesus. He also heals the sick and raises people from the dead. Even more telling, he travels to Jerusalem and goes on trial in Rome, where he is declared innocent three times. In addition, Acts begins by reviewing the Gospel, both works are addressed to Theophilus, and scrolls had limited space. Long works had to be divided.

The author of Luke is often thought of as the New Testament's historian. As is evident from the discussion above, the methods of ancient and modern historians differ quite considerably. Rather than collect objective facts, the author of Acts creates stories of Peter and Paul patterned after stories about Jesus. As we saw with the way in which the Old Testament was used in the last chapter, this patterning practice was common to New Testament writing.

One possible reason for Luke's writings was to exonerate the Romans for the crucifixion of Jesus. In the Gospel, Pilate acquits Jesus (23:22), and the Roman centurion declares him to be a righteous man (24:47). In Acts, the first pagan convert is a Roman centurion (see chapter 10), and it is the Jews who deliver Paul to Rome. At his trial, Paul is declared to be an innocent man (Acts 26:31). When his ship wrecked in a hurricane, Paul was saved by a Roman centurion (Acts 27:43).

Luke has a higher opinion of the disciples than Mark. He omits the stories of Jesus rebuking Peter (Mark 8:33), James and John's request for special positions in the kingdom (Mark 10:35–40), and the disciples' flight at Jesus' arrest (Mark 14:49). Omission was a way for an editor to put his spin on the Jesus story. In addition, in Luke the disciples stand by Jesus at his trials (Luke 22:28).

Of greater importance, Luke is a Gospel for the poor, the sick, those who are enslaved, those crippled by economic injustice, women, and those who are otherwise excluded. The Gospel articulates a vision of love and forgiveness for enemies. Jesus dines with his enemies (the Pharisees), he makes a hero of a traditional Jewish enemy (the good Samaritan), and he prays for his executioners (23:34). Luke's God is loving, kind, generous, and forgiving. The beauty of Jesus' vision couldn't be more clearly expressed.

GOSPEL FICTIONS: THE VIRGIN BIRTH STORIES OF MATTHEW AND LUKE COMPARED

In previous chapters, I have written about the data problem as it relates to ancient biography. Historical data, at least by modern standards, did not exist. There were no newspaper reports of great events in which the character under study participated. No TV interviews, and very few letters written either by the famous personage or letters about him. Ancient biographies were for the most part written many years after the person under study had died.

As a result of this lack of data, ancient biography was made up, to a large extent, by what we moderns would label as fictional story. The New Testament Gospels are no exception. Because this is a difficult premise for most Christians to accept, I want to make the point in a way that is beyond dispute by comparing the virgin birth stories in Matthew and Luke. I also want to again make the point that fiction is used in ancient biography to make important points about the identity of the person under study. Throughout the four Gospels, the fictional stories tell us a lot about Jesus' character, teachings, and mission, which the Gospel writers could not do if they had to rely on historical data that unfortunately did not exist.

The starting point to understanding the virgin birth stories in Matthew (1:18—2:23) and Luke (1:3—2:39) is to read them both carefully. When you do this, write down the main events in each story. Here is what I find when I go through this process.

In Matthew, the story begins with Mary and Joseph residing in Bethlehem. We quickly learn that Mary is with child as a result of some mysterious intervention by the Holy Spirit. Jesus is born in Bethlehem and visited by wise men. Because it was believed that a king of the Jews had been born, the current king, Herod, is threatened. He instructs the wise men to go to Bethlehem to locate Jesus and to report back to him where Jesus can be found so he can visit him and pay his respects. The wise men find Jesus by following a star, which seems to wander around in the universe. While with the family, the wise men offer gifts and have a dream telling them to return home a different way to avoid reporting to Herod.

Soon after they leave, Joseph has a dream telling him to escape to Egypt with Mary and Jesus. In anger and frustration because he was unable to locate the baby Jesus, Herod kills all male children in the surrounding area under two years of age. When Herod dies, an angel again appears to Joseph, informing him it is now safe to leave Egypt. The family travels to Nazareth.

In Luke, the story begins with Zechariah and Elizabeth, the parents of John the Baptist. Elizabeth conceives John the Baptist as a result of a miracle. In this case, God solves a fertility problem. The angel Gabriel explains to Mary that she will also have a child, conceived by the Holy Spirit. Mary visits her cousin Elizabeth. She sings the Magnificat, and John is born. The story now moves to the birth of Jesus in earnest. Caesar Augustus orders a census, which causes Mary and Joseph to make the trip from Nazareth to Bethlehem. Note that they reside in Nazareth. Mary gives birth while in Bethlehem at an inn, witnessed by shepherds. Jesus is circumcised at the temple, and the family returns to Nazareth.

Most Christians do not make such an outline. They conflate elements from both stories, and this composite picture is reinforced every Christmas when the Christmas pageant is performed in their church. However, if you are honest and objective in your examination of the two stories, it jumps out at you that the two stories have nothing in common. One is the story of the birth of a king with a star wandering around the universe, wise men visiting, children dying, and a trip to Egypt. The story in Luke is about the birth of a Palestinian peasant in a simple inn with shepherds in attendance and a quick turn-around home to Nazareth. One of these stories must be fiction. They cannot both be true. This is an important insight because it demonstrates that fictional accounts do in fact occur in the New Testament.

In fact, both stories are fiction. Why? To begin with, Paul never mentions a virgin birth in any of his letters. Paul is one of the greatest salesmen in history. If a virgin birth happened, he would have proclaimed it in every letter he wrote. Instead, Paul hints in both Romans (1:3–4) and Galatians (4:4) that the birth of Jesus occurred through normal human processes.

The Gospel of Luke

Mark never mentions a virgin birth. John also fails to mention it. The author of John suggests in chapter 6 that Jesus was born through normal human processes. In chapter 1, he indicates that Jesus was born in Nazareth (1:45–56). (See also John 7:42.) The virgin birth of Jesus is nowhere mentioned in a history of the period nor in any other New Testament document. Think about the claim: virgin birth. It's an amazing one with no independent historical confirmation. In all of world literature, the claim is made only in Matthew and Luke.

> Surely this is Jesus son of Joseph, whose mother and father we know. (John 6:42)

There are also historical problems with the two stories. The census mentioned in Luke never took place. The creator of the story uses it as a device to get Mary to Bethlehem so that the birth will confirm the prophecy of Micah (5:2)—an example of prophecy creating history, a practice I pointed out in the discussion regarding the use of the Old Testament for story creation in the last chapter. To repeat, the worldwide census never took place. There was a smaller one in Syria, however, when Jesus was ten.

Can you imagine an eight-month pregnant woman walking five or six days to get to Bethlehem? How about the star that wanders around the universe or the wise men who make a long journey to honor the birth of a Galilean peasant? These elements of Matthew's story stretch my imagination.

Bethlehem was seven miles from Jerusalem, the home of Herod. Why did Herod have to ask wise men for help in locating Jesus in this tiny village? And then there's the killing of all those children. History reports that Herod killed a few of his own kids, but there is no record of an atrocity like the one described in Matthew.

Finally, stories of miraculous births were common in ancient literature for great men. Such stories were written for Moses, Samuel, John the Baptist, Apollonius of Tyana, Alexander the Great, Romulus, Augustus Caesar to name a few. Do we believe these stories?

With the fact of fictional creation established, let's move on to what is most important. What were these stories telling people in the first century about Jesus? In the last chapter, I demonstrated how the virgin birth story in Matthew signaled the coming of the new Moses. In Luke, Jesus' birth was about the coming of Israel's last prophet, the one who would announce the imminent coming of God's kingdom. A detailed analysis of Luke's characterization of Jesus as Israel's last prophet is undertaken in the next section of the chapter.

These stories also communicate to first-century residents the type of messiah Jesus would be. The story of Moses in Exodus demonstrated the gods of Egypt had no power. The birth of Jesus in Matthew sent the same message. Herod was exposed as a king with no power. He tried all kinds of evil tricks to get rid of Jesus, but Jesus won. Herod could not defeat Jesus. The old order was discredited. The new age was dawning.

In Luke, the birth of Jesus tells us what the new order will look like. The last will be first. This will not be a kingdom where greed, power, and the imposition of one's will over another are the rule of the day. This will be a kingdom where the poor, widows, and orphans are the ones advantaged. It will be a kingdom that is inclusive, focused on economic and social justice and nonviolence.

Matthew's story also tells us that Jesus is Immanuel, the name that designates God is with us (1:23). Jesus was born with this sacred presence existing within him. He is a new creation.[2]

Finally, both stories answer an important question for the communities of faith for which each evangelist writes. When did Jesus become the Son of God? For both Matthew and Luke, this took place at birth. For Mark, Jesus became Son of God at his baptism with John in the Jordan River (Mark 1:9–11). In John's Gospel, Jesus was the incarnate Son of God who was with God from the beginning of time (John 1:1–2).

If we apply modern standards of history to these two stories, we miss these crucial points about Jesus. To try to fit these stories into history is to violate the purpose of each author. The point for us is to let the meanings of the stories sink in, to see Jesus as God with us, to think about and try to experience a kingdom for the

2. Van Ham, *Liberating Birth of Jesus*.

poor and the have-nots in society. Treated in this way, both stories can be transforming.[3] This is how ancient biography was written. A fictional story was created to convey information about the identity, character, and greatness of the person under study.

THE LAST PROPHET

The first thing you notice about Luke's virgin birth story is all the talk about prophecy. John the Baptist is born and is labeled the Prophet of the Most High (1:76). Simeon prophesied that Jesus will be a sign rejected (2:33-35). Anna adds her prophetic view that Jesus will be responsible for the deliverance of Jerusalem (2:38). All this material is unique to Luke, which points to Luke's central purpose. That purpose is to paint a picture of the Jesus of history as Israel's last prophet who announces the imminent coming of God's kingdom.[4]

The story of Jesus' miraculous birth is inspired by the story of Samuel's birth, a prophet. Compare Luke 1:18—2:23 and 1 Sam 1:1—2:11. In the two stories, a devout Jewish woman gives birth to a son by miraculous means. The women respond by praising God in song—the song of Hannah in 1 Sam 2:1-10 and the Magnificat in Luke 1:46-55. The two songs have remarkable parallels. They both exalt those who are humble, lowly, and oppressed.

The story of Jesus at the temple when he was twelve years old (2:41-50) is only in Luke. It echoes the life of the prophet Samuel. The story is about a precocious kid with a sense of vocation and wisdom well beyond his years. Again, what you see here is the use of the Old Testament to create a story about Jesus.

We have referred previously to Jesus' first sermon at Nazareth where he is rejected by both family and neighbors. Luke (4:16-30) adds two stories about the prophets Elijah and Elisha to Mark's story. These prophets are not sent to Israel but to the gentiles. God has rejected Israel for turning against him. Against this background,

---

3. Van Ham, *Liberating Birth of Jesus*.
4. Ehrman, *New Testament*, 105-10.

Jesus' message is clear. He too is a prophet. Because the Jews have rejected him, he will take his message to the gentiles.

As I pointed out with Mark, this is a fictional story. Jesus is depicted as preaching in a synagogue, a structure that didn't exist in Nazareth until two hundred years after Jesus' death.[5] Luke's story mentions an enraged crowd who responds to Jesus' message by trying to throw him off a cliff. Nazareth in the first century was a tiny place consisting of, maybe, seventy-five families. There would not be enough people to form a crowd. It is apparent that Luke knew little about Galilean geography and was therefore not an eyewitness to these events.

There are two miracle stories in chapter 7 that are most revealing. The stories have close parallels to miracle stories about Elisha and Elijah. Compare Luke 7:1–10 with 2 Kgs 5:1–14. In the story in 2 Kings, Elisha heals the Syrian general through the intercession of a young Jewish girl. In Luke, Jesus heals the slave of a gentile centurion through the intercession of Jewish elders. Luke has patterned his miracle story on a similar story about Elisha.

Continue your reading with Luke 7:11–17 and 1 Kgs 17:17–24. In the story in 1 Kings, Elijah brings back to life the son of a widow. In Luke, Jesus brings back to life the son of a widow. Both stories end with the words "and he gave him to his mother." Luke's point in this chapter is that both Elijah and Elisha are prophets, and prophets perform miracles. Jesus is also a prophet who performs miracles. The crowd witnessing the second miracle sees the connection immediately, and shouts out, "A great prophet has appeared among us" (7:17).

In chapter 13, Jesus claims to be a prophet and indicates he will die in Jerusalem. Luke has a special focus on Jerusalem, the city of prophets. He mentions the city thirty-three times, more than the other three Gospels combined. Jesus' resurrection meeting with the disciples takes place in Jerusalem (24:13–43), and he counsels the disciples to remain in Jerusalem after his death.

---

5. Crossan and Reed, *Excavating Jesus*, 25–26.

But for today and tomorrow and the next day I must go on, since it would not be right for a prophet to die outside Jerusalem. (Luke 13:33)

There are some interesting details of Jesus' death that are unique to Luke. As I pointed out in discussing Mark (15:37), the veil at the temple is torn down the middle as Jesus dies. In Luke (22:46), the temple veil is torn not as Jesus dies but as darkness comes over the land, a symbol of prophetic judgment.

The death of Jesus does not have the significance it does in the other Gospels. Luke's Gospel is not a theology of the cross. There is no mention of Jesus giving his life for many. The point of Jesus' death was his innocence. One of those crucified with him proclaims his innocence as does the centurion (23:44–49). Jesus dies the innocent death of a prophet. In death Jesus also displays his obedience. He implements God's plan as a stoic, as his last words attest: "Father, into your hands I commit my spirit" (23:46).

In Luke, Jesus is born as a prophet, he teaches and heals like one, and he dies like one. As Israel's last prophet, he announces the fulfillment of the Jewish religion and the coming kingdom of God on earth. The editor of Luke most likely takes a story performed several times by a public storyteller, makes changes to suit his purposes, and then places the story in his Gospel.

THE ORAL TRADITION ILLUSTRATED

In chapter 1, I introduced the important topic of the oral tradition and pointed out that the editors of the Gospels organized their portrayal of Jesus by story type rather than chronology. Gospel writers created stories about Jesus from written collections of similar stories. Such an organization scheme ignored a chronological progression found in historical presentations. Another interesting characteristic of the oral tradition is that stories changed as they were told and retold in different settings.

A good example of the details of a story being changed as it is told in different settings is the story of Jesus healing the son of a royal official (John 4:46-53). The official seeks Jesus out himself, and Jesus heals the son from a distance. Matthew tells the same story, but the one sick and dying is not the official's son, but his servant. Because of the official's great belief in Jesus' healing powers, Jesus heals him from a distance (Matt 8:5-13). Again, Luke tells the same story about the healing of the official's servant, but instead of seeking out Jesus himself, the official sends some Jewish elders (Luke 7:1-10).

The parables are the best remembered of Jesus' stories. They provide a wealth of evidence of detail changes as a story moves along the oral tradition highway. These stories are original, colorful, and dramatic. Yet, while the same story may appear in two Gospels, there are often significant differences between them produced by the telephone game problem and the fact that Gospel writers invent details to narrate a complete story and to spin a story to suit their purposes.

Take the parable of the wedding feast in Matthew (22:1-14) and the story of the uninvited guests who make excuses in Luke (14:15-24) as an example. In Matthew's story, a king gives a feast to celebrate his son's wedding. He sends out his servants to invite the guests. The guests all make excuses for not being able to attend. In a rage, the king kills those who spurned his invitation and destroys the town. He then instructs his servants to go out and invite everyone they see.

In Luke's story, a wealthy man has a feast to which he invites guests who make excuses for not being able to attend. The man gets mad (though no one is killed) and tells his servant to invite others. The two stories have different details, different guests, and different excuses, but the basic story the two editors report is the same.

The editors also add their own theological spin to their stories. In Matthew, after the first round of guests turns him down, the king invites anyone who cares to come. The story ends with the line "for many are called, but few are chosen" (22:14). This is part of Matthew's salvation by good works theme. You get into heaven by doing good works. Few will measure up.

In Luke, for the second round of guests, the host invites the poor, the lame, the blind. Social outcasts and the disadvantaged are a central focus of Luke's Gospel. After inviting this group, he opens it up to anyone, i.e., gentiles, another central focus of his Gospel. The kingdom of God is opening up to them. The details Luke adds to provide context for the story were carefully chosen to illustrate his favorite themes.

Read these two parables carefully to experience the point about the differences caused by the oral tradition. You might also want to compare Matt 25:14–30 and Luke 19:11–27, the parables of talents and pounds; and Matt 7:24–27 and Luke 6:47–49, the parable at the end of the Sermon on the Mount. A careful comparison of each pair shows a common core for each story with many different details as a result of the passing along of the story through the oral tradition as the playing of the telephone game would suggest.

Jesus was fond of using punch lines—short, pithy insights about life that were easy to remember. These punch lines were floating around in the oral tradition. Gospel writers attached them to the end of a story. What you end up with is different stories with the same punch line added at the end.

"Anyone who exalts himself will be humbled, anyone who humbles himself will be exalted." Read Luke 14:7–11, Luke 18:9–14, and Matt 23:1–12. In these three examples, you have different stories with the punch line "anyone who exalts himself . . ." added at the end.

Again, "many who are first will be last, and the last first." Read Matt 19:30, Matt 20:1–16, Luke 13:30, and Mark 9:35. The same pattern is evident with different stories and the same punch line ending the story. This situation happens again and again within the Gospels, a product of the oral tradition and the fact of editorial creation. In each case, a discrete unit from the tradition was taken (the core story), details were added to complete the story, and then a punch line, floating independently within the tradition, was included for effect.

The examples above point out that Gospel writing was, in part, a cut and paste job. Sometimes this job was not done well. Read the parable in Luke about the unscrupulous judge and the unfortunate widow (18:1–8). This parable ends with the idea that justice will be done speedily. Then, out of the blue, this line follows: "But when the Son of Man comes, will he find any faith on earth?" This line has no relation to the parable. It was pasted on to the last line of the parable, most likely by a scribe from the early church in the copying process, for no apparent reason I can discern except to make clear the church's position that Jesus became the Son of Man following the resurrection.

This analysis of the oral tradition demonstrates again that Gospel writing was a very human endeavor. Storytellers and final editors were human beings with their biases and their own agendas that significantly affected the pictures of Jesus they created.

RESURRECTION STORIES

There is no Christianity without the resurrection of Jesus. We need to explain how a Galilean peasant from the tiny village of Nazareth started a movement that was able to survive the Great War, relocate in the Hellenistic world, and three hundred years later become the dominant religion in the Roman world. Some dramatic events must have taken place. When we examine how the resurrection was developed in the New Testament, however, it becomes evident that these events did not include a physical return to life.

To begin with, as I suggested in discussing the passion narrative, it is very unlikely there was a physical body to resurrect. Almost certainly Jesus' body was devoured by animals as he was dying on the cross. The Romans didn't allow burial following crucifixions. Roman soldiers guarded crosses so that bodies couldn't be removed. The goal was to have the dead body devoured by an animal. The point was to make death on a cross so horrible it would act as a deterrent for people thinking of challenging Rome. Thousands of Jews were crucified around Jerusalem during the Roman colonial period with only one body discovered by archeologists indicating a crucified victim was buried.⁶

When we examine Paul's view of this event, it is clear he too rejects the idea of the physical resurrection of Jesus. This is significant because Paul was the first one to write about Jesus' resurrection. Paul insists flesh and blood do not inherit the kingdom of heaven. Paul never talks of a two-step process where Jesus walks the earth first and then ascends to heaven. Jesus dies as a flesh and blood human being, and God raises him as a spiritual body to heaven. Jesus never physically meets with people on earth after the crucifixion.

On the Damascus road, Paul sees Jesus in heaven. It is a vision experience. Read Acts 9:1–9 and Acts 26:12–17. In Acts, Paul specifically states his resurrection experience was based on a vision.

> Then I said: Who are you, Lord? And the Lord answered, "I am Jesus and you are persecuting me. But get up and stand on your feet, for I have appeared to you for this reason: to appoint you as my servant, and as witness of this vision in which you have seen me, and of others in which I shall appear to you." (Acts 26:15–17)

In 2 Cor 12:1–7, Paul talks about his visionary trip to heaven. In 1 Corinthians, Paul insists his experience was the same as the experiences of the disciples. Please read that sentence a second time. Remember also that Paul has his encounter with Jesus long after the crucifixion and the alleged ascension. As a result, he could not have had a physical encounter with Jesus. Finally, Paul met with James and Peter in Jerusalem for fifteen days, three years following his Damascus encounter. They obviously discussed the resurrection. While the Jesus movement in Jerusalem criticized Paul's views on admitting gentiles into the faith and the role of Jewish law in the gaining of salvation, you never hear of disputes concerning the resurrection.

> He appeared first to Cephas and secondly to the Twelve. Next, he appeared to more than five hundred brothers at

---

6. See Crossan and Reed, *Excavating Jesus*, 245–46.

the same time, most of whom are still alive, though some have died; then he appeared to James, and then to all the apostles; and last of all he appeared to me too. (1 Cor 15:4-8)

The other problem with the physical resurrection of Jesus is that the Gospel stories describing it are weak. There are three Gospel stories of the physical resurrection of Jesus. As I pointed out in commenting on the last eleven verses in Mark's Gospel, Mark's resurrection story (16:9-20) was written by a scribe and not Mark's final editor. Ninety-five percent of New Testament scholars take this position. It is nothing more than a weak summary of the other three stories.

There are major problems with the three remaining stories. There are lots of minor differences in the stories, which you can read about in the scholarly literature on the subject or learn for yourself by reading the three stories and listing the events in each.[7] The differences are readily apparent. What follows is a discussion of the big problems.

The first one is the evangelists do not agree as to where the resurrection takes place. Matthew places it on a mountain in Galilee (28:16-20) and Luke at a home in Jerusalem (24:33-43). The distance between these two points of reference is a five- or six-day walk. John agrees with Luke regarding the Jerusalem home (20:19-29) but adds a resurrection encounter on the shores of Lake Tiberias in Galilee (21:1-19). No other Gospel mentions this encounter at the lake, an amazing omission if eyewitnesses authored these accounts.

> Later on Jesus showed himself again to the disciples. It was by the sea of Tiberias. (John 21:1-2)

Some try to reconcile these different accounts by positing Jesus first appeared to the disciples in Jerusalem and only later in Galilee. Unfortunately, Luke's story makes such a solution impossible. According to Luke, Jesus appeared to his disciples in Jerusalem and then instructed them to remain there after his ascension

---

7. For a detailed discussion of these differences, see Spong, *Resurrection*.

The Gospel of Luke

(Luke 24:36–50). Discrepancies of this magnitude are hard to forgive. We are talking about the most spectacular event ever alleged to have taken place in human history. Where was President Kennedy assassinated? Few people living in America in 1963 would have differing views about that.

According to Matthew's account of this event, as Jesus dies on the cross, Jewish holy men rise from the grave and walk around Jerusalem. They appear to many people. No other Gospel mentions this amazing event. Can you imagine eyewitnesses, or historians for that matter, missing it? It is not reported in any history of the period.[8] From the silence of history on these remarkable claims, I must confess to having doubts that they took place.

> At that, the veil of the Temple was torn in two from top to bottom; the earth quaked, the rocks were split; the tombs opened and the bodies of many holy men rose from the dead, and these, after the resurrection, came out of the tombs, entered the Holy City and appeared to a number of people. (Matt 27:51–54)

There is a related problem. The only accounts of the physical resurrection of Jesus appear in the Christian Gospels. Why do historians of the period miss this spectacular event? There were several such historians in a position to report it.

Most important for me, and this is an original insight, is the fact that only a small group of people were able to witness this event—the disciples and a few women. All the Gospel stories agree on this point. Peter in Acts clearly states the resurrection was for a small, select group, chosen by God. What is at stake is human salvation, a gift granted to those who proclaim Jesus as their savior. The way these stories are written makes Christianity into a small, exclusive club because the vast majority of Jews living in Jerusalem at this time were prevented from encountering this great event. This missed opportunity makes it far less likely for them to confess Jesus as their savior. Can you imagine a God of love limiting

---

8. The silence of history on the Jesus of history is a well established fact. A good general discussion of this problem can be seen in Ehrman, *Jesus: Apocalyptic Prophet*, 55–64.

salvation to such a small group of people? I cannot. A God of love would have had the resurrected Jesus shake hands with every resident in Jerusalem.

> Yet three days afterward God raised him to life and allowed him to be seen, not by the whole people but only by certain witnesses God had chosen beforehand. (Acts 10:41)

As a result of these many problems, the only logical conclusion is that the physical resurrection stories are fictional accounts. So the key question for this book becomes why these fictional accounts were written. There is no question that the close followers of Jesus had a real sense of his continuing presence with them. The Gospel writers were absolutely convinced Jesus had survived the crucifixion in some way and was alive in heaven as the Son of Man. The problem is they had no reliable historical evidence of what happened following the crucifixion. In order to explain Jesus' continued existence in heaven, they invented stories to get him there. The creation of physical resurrection stories was one way to solve that problem. That is how ancient biographies were written.

LUKE'S TRAVEL NARRATIVE

Luke's travel narrative comes in the central section of the Gospel from 9:51 to 19:48. Travel narratives are a frequent occurrence in ancient biographies. The narrative begins with the statement that Jesus resolutely turned his face toward Jerusalem because his time had drawn near (9:51) and ends with his entry into Jerusalem where he teaches at the temple (19:48).

The narrative is a fictional device created by the editor to provide the listener with information about Jesus. Very few details on the actual journey are given. The narrative moves from one saying of Jesus to another. In many ways, the narrative reminds one of Matthew's discourses, although the sayings of Jesus in Luke have no established order. They are presented randomly.

The sayings come from Q and Luke's own sources (L). There are several teachings like the one where the disciples ask Jesus when the kingdom will come. In responding, Jesus provides a fascinating answer, again suggesting the kingdom will be centered in Israel.

> The coming of the kingdom of God does not admit of observation and there will be no one to say, "Look, it is here! Look, it is there!" For, look, the kingdom of God is among you. (Luke 17:20-21)

The teaching on the great commandment to love God and your neighbor is also given in the narrative (10:27).

There are several parables which are both unique to Luke and loved by Christians. These include the good Samaritan (10:29-37), the prodigal son (15:11-32), and the rich man and Lazarus (16:19-31). The parables help define the kingdom of God and characterize the God of Israel as loving and forgiving.

Finally, there are several sayings that echo Matthew's five discourses. These include the hardship of an apostolic calling (9:57-61), the mission of the disciples (10:1-16), and the teaching on brotherly correction (17:3-4). This travel narrative has nothing to do with history. It's a device created by the editor that is all about Jesus' identity, his mission, and his teachings. That's how ancient biographies were written.

CONCLUSION

From the discussion introducing the chapter, we learned Luke's Gospel was written about the same time as Matthew (85-90 CE), and from similar sources—Mark, Q, and his own (L). Like ancient writers generally, Luke never cites his sources, copies directly, rearranges material freely, never uses quotations, and has no qualms about putting words in Jesus' mouth.

There is a general consensus among scholars that one reason Luke wrote his Gospel was to exonerate Rome for the death of Jesus. The Jewish elite was responsible. In Luke's version of the passion narrative, Pilate acquits Jesus (23:13-24) and the Roman centurion who witnessed the death of Jesus declared him to be a righteous man (23:47). The problem was not with Rome but with the Jewish leaders in Jerusalem.

Luke's picture of the historical Jesus as Israel's last prophet most likely came from a long-standing performance of a storyteller. Like Matthew, Luke also wrote to improve Mark. He corrected Mark's grammar and had a more positive view of the disciples. He was also less confrontational with the Pharisees. He corrected the confusion over the vote in the Sanhedrin to condemn Jesus to death by keeping Joseph as a member and claiming he voted against convicting Jesus (23:50–51). The verdict was no longer seen as unanimous as the Gospel of Mark claims. Again, like Matthew, the final editor uses subtle changes to make these points. He was also a skilled writer who created a Gospel to answer questions that were important to his community. Finally, like Matthew, the editor of Luke's Gospel creatively put together his different sources to create a Gospel that spoke to his community and suited his purposes.

One of the great challenges in understanding the New Testament Gospels is that they all have contradictions. Because Luke's are particularly glaring, that will be our focus for the remainder of this section.

In his Gospel, Luke writes that Jesus ascended to heaven three days after being crucified (24:51). In Acts, the ascension took place forty days following the crucifixion. During this forty-day period, Jesus made continuous appearances to his close followers (Acts 1:3). This discrepancy is too great to explain away, assuming the two works were written by the same author, an author who is highly intelligent as his writing skills demonstrate.

A similar problem exists with the resurrection. Luke's portrayal of the resurrection in his Gospel is the most physical of all the Gospel accounts. Jesus tells his disciples to touch his body, and he eats with them (24:36–43). In writing about Paul's encounter with the resurrected Jesus in Acts, it is clear that Paul saw and heard Jesus in heaven through a series of vision experiences. There was no physical encounter on earth. Jesus had been raised to heaven. If Paul is to be believed, you cannot explain this difference by arguing that after physically meeting with his disciples in Jerusalem Jesus met with Paul at a later date through a series of vision experiences. According to Paul, his resurrection encounter with Jesus was the same as the disciples (1 Cor 15:3–8).

There is also confusion over who the historical Jesus was. As I pointed out earlier in this chapter, a central focus of Luke's Gospel was to portray Jesus as a prophet. He is also portrayed as the Jewish Messiah, a king from the house of David (1:32, 1:68–71, 2:4). He arrives in Jerusalem for the Passover celebration as a king (19:38). But then in 12:8–12, Jesus declares himself to be the Son of Man. See also 9:26, 21:27, and 22:69. The Son of Man was thought to be a preexistent, divine being. Prophets and kings were human beings.

Finally, there is confusion over who will become part of the kingdom of God after the resurrection. Luke in the Gospel argues that God has rejected the Jews and the kingdom of God will be inherited by gentiles. Simeon prophesies that Jesus will be a sign of God's disapproval of Israel (2:33–35). When Jesus preaches his first sermon in Nazareth, Luke adds to Mark's story. It is important to pay attention to material unique to a Gospel writer. It signals an important theme. In this case, the added material includes stories of Elijah and Elisha giving up on Israel and going to the gentiles. The story of the narrow gate is about the rejection of the Jewish nation and God replacing them with gentiles (17:22–30). Despite this focus in the Gospel, the author of Acts has stories of Jews coming over to Jesus by the thousands. (See Acts 2:41, 4:4, 6:7, and 21:20.)

I can offer two explanations for these contradictions. First, the final editors, writing many years after these events in a setting far removed from Palestine, knew very little about the historical Jesus. The most honest characterization of the historical Jesus I have come across in all of my reading on the subject comes from Morton Smith. Smith compares Jesus to a subatomic particle. Physicists employ the strongest microscopes in their laboratories to try to locate the parts of the atom, but they are too tiny for them to see. They escape all positive identification. It is only possible to know these particles by the effect they exert on the particles around them.⁹

Like a subatomic particle, Jesus is best known by his effect. The truth is that history can't find the historical Jesus, as I pointed out in chapter 1. On the other hand, the resurrection produced a profound effect. The followers of Jesus were left with a deep sense of his living presence. The problem is that it is very difficult to translate this sense of presence into historical details, which helps us understand much of the confusion described above. Jesus was experienced with God in heaven so he must have ascended. When that happened, opinions differed. Was it three days or forty? Did Jesus rise from the dead as a physical body who met with his close followers before ascending to heaven, or did he ascend directly to heaven following his crucifixion, appearing to his closest followers through vision experiences? Again, opinions differed.

The conflicting fictional stories that developed around these events were not written to lie about Jesus or to inflate his reputation in some way. They were written by people who deeply believed in the main point of the story they were creating. The problem was that they lacked credible historical evidence with which to communicate their deeply held beliefs.

The second explanation is that the final product of Luke, as with the other three Gospels, was produced by committee. As I explained previously, ancient writers do not copyright their work. There is no strong sense of ownership. Scribes felt free to add or subtract when copying a text. The early church was responsible for adding the Son of Man material to Mark, which was adopted by Matthew and Luke. We have no idea how much the Gospel version we possess was worked over by scribes, but that clearly was the case. There is a one-hundred year gap between the original version of Luke and the earliest text we have.¹⁰ That left plenty of

---

9. John Dominic Crossan quotes an extended passage by Morton Smith that makes this point in his book *The Historical Jesus*. See xxvii.

10. The problem of finding the original version of the text for each of the four Gospels is discussed at length in Ehrman's book *Misquoting Jesus*. See 57–58 and 71–100.

time for scribes to add material they deemed to be important, material that may have helped to create some of the contradictions described above.

Despite these problems, the message of Luke shines bright. God is portrayed as big-hearted and forgiving. The Gospel tone is one of optimism and joy. The word "joy" occurs more frequently in Luke than the other three Gospels combined. Jesus is portrayed as possessing a special concern for the oppressed—the poor, the sick, women, slaves, orphans, widows, lepers. The last shall be first. He is radically concerned with inclusion and the practice of nonviolence. For these reasons, Luke's Gospel presents a picture of Jesus that can be transforming if Christian believers make the decision to organize their lives around Luke's vision.

5

The Gospel of John

GOSPEL MECHANICS

AT FIRST BLUSH, THE Gospel of John is a mess. It is filled with text problems, and there are so many contradictions that a good case can be made it was written by a committee. However, once you dig below the surface things look much better. The main message discussed in the next section comes through loud and clear.[1]

You can't read the Gospel of John without noticing how different it is from the Synoptics. The Gospel is organized around a three-year ministry for Jesus rather than the one-year ministry in the Synoptics. Jesus sets out three times for Jerusalem for the Passover festival (2:13, 5:1, and 7:10). The author also seems to know a great deal more about Palestinian geography and the operations of Jewish institutions and customs than his colleagues who wrote the Synoptic Gospels. As I pointed out previously, the meeting of the Sanhedrin in John's story to condemn Jesus takes place well before the Passover celebration. Jewish law prevented it from meeting during Passover as depicted in the Synoptic Gospels.

---

1. For the most part the scholarly literature agrees with what appears in this section and the one that follows. I am particularly indebted to Anderson, *Riddles of the Fourth Gospel*; Brown, *Gospel According to John*; Barrett, *Gospel According to St. John*; Smith, *Theology of the Gospel of John*; Newbigin, *Light Has Come*; and Burge, *Anointed Community*.

The Gospel of John

If you read John with some degree of objectivity and attention, you will note there are no parables, no exorcisms, no messianic secret, no birth story, no temptation in the wilderness, no Sermon on the Mount, no baptism by John, no transfiguration, no Gethsemane. As I pointed out in the chapter on Mark, John's passion narrative is considerably different from Mark and Luke. It is apparent the author of John chose differently from the oral tradition than the other Gospel writers. The fact that the Gospel is so unique demonstrates how rich in stories the oral tradition was. The writers of the New Testament Gospels had many stories to choose from.

Irenaeus, a second-century bishop, claims the Gospel was written by John, the beloved disciple, who lived to a great age in Ephesus. The Gospel claims such an eyewitness (21:24). There are several historical problems with this claim, however. To begin, the New Testament knows nothing of John living in Ephesus. In Gal 2:9, Paul has him living in Jerusalem. Acts also shows no awareness of John living in Ephesus. Papias, another second-century church leader, concurs with this view. He claims John was killed in Jerusalem with his brother.

In addition, one has to ask if the disciple John could have survived the Great War and lived into his nineties. The general consensus is that the Gospel was written between 90 and 100 CE. As I mentioned in discussing this issue with Mark, the average lifespan of a first-century male living in Palestine was thirty years of age.

Finally, the author of Acts describes John as an illiterate Galilean peasant (Acts 4:13). As I will point out throughout this chapter, the Gospel of John is one of theological brilliance. Would an illiterate peasant have the ability to write a philosophical Gospel? As I have noted before, it was common to name a piece of writing to honor someone in the ancient world. That's what is most likely to have happened here. The Gospel was named in honor of John, the beloved disciple.

One thing that is interesting about this Gospel is we do have some evidence to support the date of writing between 90 and 100 CE. There is a reference to Jews being expelled from the synagogue in 9:23. The dispute between the Pharisees and the Jesus movement for control of Judaism did not heat up until the mid 80s or later. Once that bitter dispute moved into full swing, there is plenty of evidence of Jewish Christians being expelled from the synagogue.

The story in chapter 9 is an interesting one about a man born blind who regains his sight by professing faith in Jesus. The man was expelled from the synagogue because he confessed Jesus as the Christ. Such a proclamation could never have taken place in 30 CE because it was well before people thought of Jesus in this way. The idea of Jesus as the Christ came several years after the crucifixion. This problem suggests at least some of the elements of the story are fictional, an idea we come back to frequently when discussing John.

Before leaving the question of dating the Gospel, it is important to point out that the date cannot be pinpointed to one year. An evangelist did not sit down to write this Gospel from his recollections as an eyewitness nor did an editor pen the Gospel from selected sources at his disposal at a specific date. The creation of John was a process with different parts coming at different times over many years.

There are many text-related problems within the Gospel. For example, in chapter 2 Jesus performs his first sign at Cana in rural Galilee. However, the final editor says in 2:23 that many people in Jerusalem came to believe in him because of the signs (plural!) he was doing. The problem here is that at this point in the story he had only performed one sign. There is no explanation about how he had traveled to Jerusalem to perform additional signs. The statement about creating believers in Jerusalem belongs in a later chapter in the Gospel.

Chapters 4, 5, 6, and 7 would make more chronological and geographical sense if they were rearranged. It makes better sense for chapters 4 and 6 to follow each other with Jesus in Galilee with chapter 5 and 7 placing him in Jerusalem. The logical progression based on Jesus' travel is for a chapter order of 4, 6, 5, and 7. Thematically, however, it makes sense for the bread theme in chapter 6 to be followed by the water theme in chapter 7.

The famous story of the adulterous woman the Pharisees want to stone with Jesus challenging them to go ahead and throw the first stone if any of them are without sin (7:57—8:11) was almost certainly added by a later editor or scribe. The language used in the story is different from the rest of the Gospel, and the story is not found in the earliest texts. There is almost universal agreement among New Testament scholars on this point. The Council of Trent, meeting from 1545 to 1563, officially voted to add the story to John's Gospel.[2]

In chapter 14 at the end of a long speech, Jesus says to his disciples: "Come now, let's go" (14:31). However, instead of leaving, Jesus gives another sermon about the true vine. This sermon takes up all of chapters 15 and 16 and is followed by his final prayer, which encompasses all of chapter 17. Jesus and his disciples don't leave until 18:1.

I have focused considerable attention on these textual problems because they illustrate one more time how the oral tradition creates a Gospel. It's a cut and paste job. Clear insertions have been made by an editor or a scribe in copying the work. Some scholars argue the Gospel was edited twice. On the other hand, the profound theological insights found in the Gospel make clear it was put together in its final form by a powerful mind.

The Gospel is organized into five parts. It begins with a Prologue (1:1–18). These eighteen verses most likely came from a Christian hymn. Most scholars believe the Prologue was an add-on by a later editor because it is so different from the rest of the Gospel. The key term of *logos* never appears again in the Gospel. The Prologue serves to introduce the Gospel. It lays out important themes the Gospel writer will take up.

The second section of the Gospel is called the Book of Signs (chapter 1:19 through chapter 12). Within this section are seven miracle stories, five of which are unique to John. Again, it is evident that the final editor picked differently from the oral tradition than his three colleagues. It is interesting that the miracle stories are used differently in John. In the Synoptic Gospels, the miracle

---

2. Brown, *Introduction to the New Testament*, 52.

stories show Jesus defeating Satan so that the kingdom of God can emerge. In John, they are used to create belief by demonstrating Jesus' extraordinary power. In the Synoptics, Jesus speaks about the coming of the kingdom of God. In John, he speaks about himself. It's all about identity.

In this section, a miracle story is followed by a long discourse by Jesus. These discourses have a distinct pattern. Most begin with a statement by Jesus that is misunderstood. Jesus then goes on to explain in a long speech the meaning of his answer. Most of these discourses have no eyewitnesses present. It is clear you don't memorize a long speech by listening to it. There were certainly no recording devices present. No one was there taking notes. So where did this material come from? What seems likely is that the editor who put this section together had a source in front of him consisting of sermons by church leaders.[3]

These sermons express the long theological reflection that the Johannine community undertook over many years regarding the nature of Jesus as the Messiah. The editor put parts of these sermons into the Gospel to provide commentary on the miracle story and attributed the words to Jesus. Long speeches were often found in ancient biography. Such speeches usually reflected the opinions of the biographer rather than the person under study.

A good example of this is the dialogue Jesus has with the Pharisee Nicodemus in chapter 3. When Nicodemus asks Jesus about what it means to be born again, Jesus goes into a long speech in giving his answer. The speech received written form seventy years after the death of Jesus. There are no eyewitnesses there, and Nicodemus was not a follower of Jesus. It is extremely unlikely he was taking notes. As a result, this speech (3:11–21) came from someone other than Jesus. The same set of circumstances occurs in the next chapter when Jesus has an extended discussion with a Samaritan woman. You will note that the Gospel writer has no qualms about inventing a speech and putting words in Jesus' mouth.

Returning briefly to the Nicodemus story, there is a misunderstanding regarding the meaning of the word "born again."

---

3. See Barrett, *Gospel According to St. John*, 26.

Nicodemus understands it as meaning to be born a second time. For Jesus, the word means to be born from above. It is a statement about grace. Jesus is saying that natural birth won't lead to eternal life, only selection by God, to be born from above. What is interesting is that this play on words is only possible in Greek where the word "born again" has two meanings. In Aramaic, the language Jesus spoke, there are two different words, one expressing born a second time and the other born from above, suggesting again that the story was invented.[4]

The third section of the Gospel is referred to as the Book of Glory (13:1—17:26). These chapters contain the Farewell Discourses (chapters 14–17). A farewell address from the person under study was a common feature of ancient biographies. In this case, the three chapters in John devoted to it contain an extended monologue by Jesus about mutual love. It's one of the most beautiful presentations in the New Testament. Its length and the fact that only the disciples were present suggest it is again the work of someone other than Jesus who had no qualms about putting words in Jesus' mouth.

On the day before Passover, Jesus and his disciples have supper together. After supper, Jesus washes the feet of the disciples as an example of how they should treat each other in a spirit of mutual care (13:1–12). The discourses begin at the supper table where Jesus speaks directly to his disciples with no one else in attendance (14:1).

In chapter 14, Jesus sums up the meaning of his life and ministry and repeats his one commandment that the disciples love one another as he has loved them (14:12). Chapter 15 revolves mostly around the church. The Christian community has replaced Israel as the meaning for the symbol of the vine. Jesus is the vine, the center of the Christian community. Individual branches are nourished by their connection to him. If a branch breaks away, it withers and dies. Chapter 16 is about the coming of the Paraclete. When Jesus dies and returns to his Father, the Paraclete will descend to nourish, lead, and teach the Christian community. The

---

4. Brown, *Gospel According to John*, 135–36.

Paraclete is the personification of Jesus' living presence within the community. This loving presence will remain with them forever. The Paraclete is what makes realized eschatology possible, a major theme in John's Gospel that is discussed in the next section. In chapter 17, Jesus prays for himself, asking God to glorify him so that he can complete his mission, and he prays for the disciples, a prayer of mutual love where the love God has for Jesus will be reflected in them.

Chapters 18 through 20 contain the passion narrative and the resurrection, which encompasses the fourth section. Finally, the last section of the Gospel, the Epilogue (chapter 21), is an add-on most likely from a scribe to exonerate Peter, who had failed Jesus during his final week in Jerusalem. The logical ending of the Gospel is John 20:31. The issues of mechanics in John are distinctive and the text problems create some complexity; but, as you will see in the next section, the Gospel is organized around two central themes, which facilitates understanding.

THE MESSAGE OF JOHN

As I just pointed out, John is a Gospel with two central themes. The first one concerns revelation. Jesus is the incarnate Son of God. The Gospel moves from one example to the next in expressing that theme. The Prologue begins, "In the beginning was the Word: the word was with God and the word was God" (1:1). Jesus is the preexistent Son of God, the divine *logos*, the Word. He was with God from the beginning of time.

Many New Testament scholars argue these ideas come from Philo of Alexandria, a contemporary of Jesus from the Roman colony in Egypt. Philo was most noted for his attempt to harmonize Greek philosophy with Judaism. As a Platonist, Philo argued that the high, transcendent God of Israel doesn't shape the world directly. Instead, God shapes the world by his Word, the divine *logos*, the firstborn of God who mediates for him. This divine *logos* is the point of contact between God and man, God's agent who created the earth and works to keep the world functioning according to God's plan. The author of the Christian hymn in the Prologue makes this point about Jesus.[5]

The key statement in the Prologue comes in 1:17. "The word was made flesh. He lived among us." John says here and throughout his Gospel that if you want to know what God is like, look at Jesus. Revelation is a central theme in John's Gospel. Note this comes at the very beginning of the Gospel. Introductions in ancient literature are just like ours. They too introduce the most important ideas that follow.

The early followers of Jesus experienced God in him. Following years of reflection on these experiences, some members of the Johannine community came to believe Jesus was God walking around on earth. The reflections led to the famous "I am" statements in John's Gospel. These statements include "I am the bread of life" (6:35); "I am the light of the world" (8:12); "before Abraham ever was, I am" (8:57); "I am the good shepherd" (10:14); and "I am the resurrection and the life" (11:25). After encountering God at the burning bush, Moses asks God for his name. God answered, "I am" (Exod 3:13–15). With his use of "I am" in the statements above, Jesus claims to be God.

So, God and Jesus are one. The Trinity comes from this Gospel, but there is another view in John that contradicts the "I am" statements cited above. Contradictions appear frequently in John. In many places in John, Jesus is not God walking around, but rather Jesus is pictured as if God was walking around. It is important to note that, for John, though Jesus and God are one, this unity is based on obedience, not essence (12:49, 17:4). Jesus does nothing on his own. He is totally dependent on God. In 14:28, Jesus says: "The Father is greater than I."

---

5. Though no direct literary relationship can be found between Philo and John, there are obvious parallels in their use of the term *logos* as the point of contact between God and man. For a discussion of the influence of Greek philosophy and Philo in particular on the Gospel of John, see Barrett, *Gospel According to St. John*, 34–41; Brown, *Gospel According to John*, lvii–lviii; and Smith, *Theology of the Gospel of John*, 10–12.

> I tell you most solemnly, the Son can do nothing by himself; he can do only what he sees the Father doing: and whatever the Father does the Son does too. (John 5:19; see also 5:30)

In this view of Jesus' relationship with God, Jesus and God are one, but this is not a unity of equal beings. By love and obedience, Jesus is one with the Father. By that same love and obedience, the Christian believer becomes one with Jesus. Mystical union is an important theme in John.

The story of Jesus in John was written to create belief. The miracle stories were not to be kept quiet as in Mark (the messianic secret), but to be broadcast for all to hear. Their purpose was to create belief. The resurrection story had a similar purpose. The word "belief" occurs ninety-eight times in John. Its combined use in the other three Gospels is thirty-four times. This is the Gospel about belief in Jesus as the Christ. Such belief leads to salvation. It is important to understand that this belief is not about adherence to certain tenets of doctrine, but rather a belief in Jesus that comes from direct experience.

John uses many images to make his point about revelation. One of the most important is light. Jesus comes into the world shining a great big light. He is the light of the world, the truth about God. To know that truth is to be set free (8:32). The editor of the Gospel uses the light image to change the idea about judgment. Because Jesus is light, people can see the light and decide for or against Jesus. If they fail to accept Jesus, they judge themselves. The idea of judgment as an end of the world event is greatly deemphasized, though its presence in places creates another contradiction. (See John 5:28–29.)

> I, the light, have come into the world, so that whoever believes in me need not stay in the dark any more. If anyone hears my words and does not keep them faithfully, it is not I who shall condemn him, since I have come not to condemn the world, but to save the world; he who rejects me and refuses my words has his judge already. (John 12:46–48)

The Gospel of John

The idea of judgment is related to the second theme in the Gospel, of realized eschatology. Eschatology encompasses ideas concerning the final events of history—end of the world stuff. Realized eschatology is the idea that the kingdom of God is here now and not some future event. This is John's explanation as to why the kingdom had not come as a promised, imminent event. There are no parables in John's Gospel because parables are about the coming of a future kingdom. There are no exorcisms in John's Gospel because they are about Jesus' battle with Satan which, when won, would bring in God's kingdom. Gospel writers freely pick and choose from the oral tradition in creating their stories. John's point was the kingdom was already here in the community of Christian believers.

In John's Gospel, eternal life means to live with God. This is possible now in a Christian community. When Jesus dies, he releases his Spirit called the Paraclete (7:39). This Spirit of Jesus creates the Christian community, a community based on mutual love, compassion, and service to neighbor. This community is found in Christian churches. While the ideas of a second coming and a final judgment are present in John, these ideas are greatly deemphasized. John's focus is on the present.

The bringing back to life of Lazarus (11:1–44) spells out this theme. It is the most amazing miracle story in the New Testament, and it is only found in John. Most Christians are familiar with the story. Lazarus has been dead for four days before Jesus brings him back to life. When Jesus tells Martha, Lazarus's sister, that Lazarus will live again, Martha replies she knows he will. He will rise on the last day. This is future eschatology—the common expectation among Christians of a final judgment and a second coming in the near future. No, Jesus tells her. I am the resurrection. If anyone believes in me, that person will have life now (11:25–26). This is realized eschatology—a central theme of John's Gospel. He uses a miracle story to make his point, a story we will see in the next section is almost certainly a fictional account. The theme of realized eschatology is expressed throughout the Gospel as the passages cited below attest.

> I tell you most solemnly, whoever listens to my words, and believes in the one who sent me, has eternal life; without being brought to judgment he has passed from death to life. I tell you most solemnly, the hour will come—in fact it is already here—when the dead will hear the voice of the Son of God, and all who hear it will live. (John 5:24–25; see also 4:34, 15:2–3, and 17:3)

Jesus cleanses the temple, signifying that he is the new dwelling place for God's presence. He will provide access to God. The temple has been replaced. This story takes place in chapter 2. John gets right to it. As you will remember, this story comes toward the end in the Synoptic Gospels. Stories about Jesus move along the oral tradition highway without context. They are isolated units with no information relating to time or place.

Jesus also replaces Tabernacles (John 7:1–39). Tabernacles is one of the three central celebrations on the Jewish religious calendar. It commemorates the fall harvest and God's providence in providing rain so that crops can grow. Jesus claims to be the source of living water. He makes claims elsewhere to be the bread from heaven celebrated at Passover. He replaces Passover too. John's Gospel has nothing to do with biography as we understand it. It's all about identity. Who is Jesus? He is the way, a way of self-giving love where the only commandment to be his follower is to love one another (15:12).

The death of Jesus was seen as an atoning sacrifice. There was an idea in first-century Palestine that the death of a virtuous person could cause God to forgive the sins of many people and spare them punishment. (See John 11:49–53.) John pictures Jesus this way—the perfect sacrifice, the lamb of God who takes away the sins of the world. Jesus dies a day earlier in John than in the Synoptic Gospels, the day of preparation, when lambs were slaughtered for use at Passover. John changed the timing of Jesus' death to make that point.

John has text problems and is riddled with contradictions: a kingdom now and in the future, God and Jesus are one and yet the Father is greater than I, judgment now and in the future, and there are others. Despite these problems, it's an amazing work of theological brilliance built around the creation of story developed after years of reflection by members of the Johannine community.

THE MIRACLE STORIES

As I pointed out introducing John, the Gospel has seven miracle stories, five of which are unique to him. The Synoptic Gospels each have a similar collection of miracle stories. These miracle stories in all four Gospels are works of fiction.

The biggest problem I have with the historicity of the miracle stories is that they assume God intervenes directly in human affairs to change an outcome. Ancients made that exact assumption. If that was true two thousand years ago, why did God stop intervening?

I find no evidence that God acts in this way. Think about the Holocaust, for example. Six million Jews prayed to the same God Christians do, asking God to intervene and save them. Instead, six million Jews died in gas chambers. No God of love who acts in history would have allowed this despicable atrocity to happen.

Fifteen years ago, my wife Lyn and I were returning to our home in the North Carolina mountains from Colorado. We stopped in rural Tennessee to get gas. Lyn does all the driving, bless her heart. Because I was tired of reading, I went inside to purchase a local newspaper to do the crossword puzzle.

There was an amazing story on the front page. A tornado had struck a trailer park in the small town a week before. The tornado hit a trailer where a young couple lived with their six-month-old son. The tornado sliced the trailer in half, leaving the couple untouched, asleep in bed.

When the couple awoke in the morning, they noticed to their horror that half of their trailer was gone along with their son. They searched frantically for him, and, forty-five minutes into the search, they found him wedged up in a tree. The little boy smiled down on them in recognition. They rescued him and found hardly a scratch. The members of the small church they attended were convinced a miracle had taken place, that God had intervened to save the little boy's life.

On page 3 of the paper, I read that the same tornado struck another town five miles down the road, leaving four people dead in its wake. Does a God of love pick and choose? Not a God I want to believe in.

Yes, there is mystery in the world. Strange things happen that are hard to explain logically. People who are prayed for survive stage four cancer, but others die who were also prayed for. Christians love to give God credit for all the good things that happen and are good at dismissing, ignoring, or finding excuses for things that don't work out well.

Like all fictional stories in the New Testament, the miracle stories were created for a purpose. As I pointed out in introducing John, his miracle stories were designed to create belief in Jesus as the Christ. The first reported miracle in John takes place in Cana where Jesus, his disciples, and his mother, Mary, attend a wedding. When Mary reports that they have run out of wine, Jesus has six waterpots filled with water that he changes into wine.

> This was the first of Jesus' signs at Cana in Galilee. He revealed his glory, and his disciples believed in him. (John 2:11)

The miracle stories were also used to make theological points. As I suggested in the last section, John uses the Lazarus story to illustrate the workings of realized eschatology. Mark uses the story of Jesus healing the blind man in two stages (8:22–26) to suggest the disciples only have a partial understanding of the nature of Jesus' messiahship. The two healings in chapter 7 of Luke make the point that Jesus was Israel's last prophet.

Think briefly about the raising of Lazarus, a man who had been dead for four days and is brought back to life. This is the most spectacular miracle story in the New Testament, and it is only reported in John. If this event happened and if eyewitnesses wrote the Gospels, this miracle would have appeared in every Gospel.

In discussing the worldview of ancient people in chapter 1, we looked at the different understanding of disease. To review briefly, people in first-century Palestine believed disease was caused by Satan invading the body. Sickness was seen as punishment for sin.

> Then some people appeared, bringing him a paralytic stretched out on a bed. Seeing their faith, Jesus said to the paralytic, "Courage my child, your sins are forgiven." (Matt 9:2; see also Luke 5:20)

Ancients had no idea of the biological causes of disease. When Jesus cures disease, he is attacking Satan, the power of evil. In doing so, he is bringing in the kingdom of God. The miracle stories were written, in part, to communicate that message. The fact that the kingdom of God never arrived and the power of evil remains a force in the world discredits both the theory of disease held in the ancient world and the fact that Jesus succeeded as a miracle worker in defeating it.

> At sunset all those who had friends suffering from diseases of one kind or another brought them to him, and laying his hands on each he cured them. Devils too came out of many people, howling. (Luke 4:40–41)

In addition, from Luke: "But if it is through the finger of God that I cast out devils, then know the kingdom of God has overtaken you" (11:20–21).

These healing miracles were also used by the Gospel writers to proclaim Jesus as the Messiah. Isaiah prophesied the signs that would become evident when the kingdom was here. You will know when the kingdom is here, according to Isaiah, when the blind see, the deaf hear, the lame walk, and the tongues of the dumb are untied (35:1–6). Mark reports a miracle for each sign. (See Mark 8:22–26, 7:31–37, 2:1–12, and 7:31–37.) Note again that the kingdom never arrived.

The nature miracles can also be understood in the same way. When Jesus calms the storm (Mark 6:47–52), he is ending the chaos of Satan and bringing in God's rule. Nature miracles were not unique to Jesus. Humans believed to have powers over the natural world included Apollonius, Pythagoras, Moses (Exod 14:15–24), Joshua (Josh 3:1–17), Elijah (1 Kgs 17:1), and Elisha (2 Kgs 2:6–13). Alexander the Great parted the Pamphylian Sea, and Xerxes, the Persian king, walked on water. Julius Caesar and Augustus calmed the sea.[6] Do we believe the miracle stories about those listed above?

It is also important to note that many miracle stories in the New Testament are based on Old Testament and Hellenistic models. As I reported in chapter 4, the two miracles in chapter 7 of Luke are based on Old Testament stories of Elisha and Elijah. The miracle of changing water into wine in chapter 2 of John is a Dionysus type miracle. Hellenism had a concept of the divine man. Its most important characteristic was that of miracle worker. Ancient believers craved the supernatural. Physical healing by miraculous means played an important role in every ancient religion in the Roman world.

Religious leaders were expected to perform miracles in the first century. It proved God was working through them. Moses, Elijah, and Elisha of Old Testament fame were known as miracle workers. In first-century Palestine, Honi the Circle-Drawer, Rabbi Hanina ben Dosa, and the pagan Apollonius of Tyana were known as miracle workers. In the New Testament, the disciples of Jesus and Paul heal the sick, cast out demons, and bring people back to life. Stories about all of these people are very similar to those about Jesus. Do we believe them?

Remember that the Gospels were written in the Hellenistic world, not the Jewish world of Palestine. As I mentioned above, the Hellenistic world had a belief in "the divine man." These figures were seen as being born through a union of god and a human being. Because of this union, they had special powers that were demonstrated in their performance of miracles. Christian missionaries may have invented miracle stories about Jesus in an attempt to show that he was a divine man like the holy men in the Hellenistic world. The biographers of Jesus knew little about his actual history, but they believed he had special powers given him by God like the

---

6. See Carter, *Jesus and the Empire of God*.

many divine men in ancient Greece and Rome. As a result, they selected stories from the oral tradition created by Christian missionaries to paint a picture of Jesus in this image of the divine man.

Never forget that fictional stories in ancient biographies were created to make a point about the hero under study that the creators of the story firmly believed. The problem was that they had no historical data to form the basis of their story. Their only alternative was to invent their own facts. To understand the writing of the Christian Gospels, we must surrender many of our modern views about historical fact and biography and try to place ourselves in the world of the first century. This was a world saturated in supernatural beliefs. If you believed Jesus was a great spiritual leader, the worldview of the first century demanded he be portrayed as a miracle worker. His performance of miracles proved God was working through him. The central question in the ancient world was not, Do miracles happen? but, Who performs them?

My favorite way to conclude this discussion is to refer to a story Bart Ehrman reports in his book *The New Testament*, under the heading "One Incredible Life." To paraphrase the story: from the beginning his mother knew he was no ordinary person. His birth was both miraculous and accompanied by supernatural signs. He was recognized as a spiritual leader from his youth. As an adult, he went from place to place preaching a message focusing on attaining spiritual goals, not material ones. He had disciples, many of whom were convinced he was the son of God. He performed miracles: healing the sick, casting out demons, raising the dead. At the end of his life, he was placed on trial by Roman authorities for crimes against the state. His life, however, was not bound by death. Some of his followers claimed he had ascended to heaven while others said he had appeared to them alive, that they had talked with him and touched him.

The remarkable life described in Ehrman's book is not Jesus of Nazareth but Apollonius of Tyana, a Pythagorean teacher and pagan holy man of the first century. His life and teachings are recorded in *The Life of Apollonius* by Philostratus.[7]

7. See Ehrman, *New Testament*, 17.

CONCLUSION

In concluding on the writing of the Gospel of John, I'm going to engage in some pure speculation. Speculation is both fun and possible when writing on New Testament topics because so little is actually known. In what follows, I will propose that the original version of the Gospel of John was a performed church service that focuses on the two central themes of revelation and realized eschatology. Because this speculation is nothing more than a well-educated guess, I will end the chapter with a more traditional interpretation of how the Gospel was written.

The service most likely takes place in a leading member of the community's home. It begins with a hymn (the Prologue, 1:1–18) that celebrates the cosmic Word made flesh. This hymn introduces the central themes of the Gospel. Jesus is declared to be God's Son, the Word made flesh (1:1). As the divine Word, Jesus is the self-expression of God. Jesus is the way, the truth, the light. John's Gospel is all about revelation, a theme the hymn proclaims.

The second part of the service comes from a performance by the resident storyteller who has in his possession a collection of preached sermons by Christian prophets. From this collection, the storyteller selects portions of the sermons that will be the subject of that day's focus. His presentation will change with each performance on a different Sunday.

Who is this guy Jesus, the storyteller asks? He is the bread of life, the pronouncement that follows the miracle of the loaves makes clear (6:35). He is the gate for the sheepfold we learn from the parable of the good shepherd in chapter 10. Anyone who enters through it will be safe, will receive eternal life, a life on earth infused with a new quality (10:7–9). He is the resurrection and the life, our storyteller thunders, the loving force behind our blessed community. He is the source of living water, the storyteller continues. Like the water he provides the Samaritan woman at the well, he will quench your thirst. This water he gives becomes a spring for the welling up of eternal life (4:10–14). What a guy, the storyteller explains, to relate to such a woman.

The third part of the service includes a dramatic presentation of the last meal Jesus shares with his disciples in Jerusalem the day before the Passover festival, a reenactment of Jesus' meeting with the disciples in the Farewell Discourses (chapters 14–17). I imagine the churchgoers adjourning to a room with tables and chairs to share bread and wine while the storyteller gently speaks about mutual love and the role the Paraclete will play in their community. He will warn the community that the world will hate them, it's nasty out there; but, within the community of Christian believers, mutual love will produce a new quality of life and enable you to endure the challenges of the world.

The church service closes with prayer that comes in chapter 17. At the conclusion of their meeting, Jesus prays telling God he has finished his work on earth and asking God to glorify him as he has glorified God. He then prays for the disciples, assuring God they belong to him. Finally, Jesus prays for later generations who will come to believe in him. The storyteller will creatively integrate these themes in a prayer that speaks to the needs of his community. At some point, most likely sometime in the late 90s, the service attained a formal written form.

If this speculative account of the original performance of John is even close to being correct, additional sections were added to the Gospel at a later date. Such additions were possible because there is no evidence of the Gospel's existence until 150 CE, leaving plenty of time for changes to be made. The first addition was the passion narrative (18:1—20:31). The source for this story was either Mark, in which case the editor of John made substantial changes, or an independent source from the oral tradition.

There were two important reasons for adding a passion narrative. When Jesus meets his disciples in the closed room in Jerusalem at the resurrection, he gave them the gift of the Holy Spirit, the force behind the Paraclete, which would guide them in their spiritual communities (20:20). The resurrection also confirms the statement of John the Baptist that Jesus was the lamb of God who takes away the sins of the world (1:29). In John, Jesus is placed on the cross a day earlier than the other three Gospels, on the day of preparation, when lambs were prepared for the Passover sacrifice. The passion narrative in John portrays Jesus' death as an atoning sacrifice.

The logical ending of the Gospel appears at 20:30–31 with the statement that the Gospel was written so that all might believe in Jesus as the Christ and as a result receive life through his name. Chapter 21, the Epilogue, presents the story of an additional resurrection encounter at the Sea of Galilee. As you read through it, you will note a major focus on Peter and his relationship with Jesus. The story was added by the church to rehabilitate Peter.

While realized eschatology is a major focus of John's Gospel, the more traditional ideas surrounding salvation as a future event also creep into the Gospel. Rudolf Bultmann argues that the references to salvation as a future event along with the rehabilitation of Peter that appears in the Epilogue were added by an editor from the early church to make John more compatible with more orthodox thinking on these issues.[8]

In defense of Bultmann, let's look at two discourses from the Book of Signs. In the story of the cure of the sick man at the pool of Bethseda (5:1–47), Jesus cures the man on the Sabbath, which creates a controversy with the Jews. Jesus' explanation further enrages them. He argues that because God worked on the Sabbath he could work on it too. In doing so he makes himself equal to God. In a long defense of his position, Jesus makes a clear statement of realized eschatology (5:24–25). Immediately following these two verses is a clear statement of a future judgment and a future salvation (5:26–30).

The same pattern is evident in the discourse following the miracle of the loaves (6:1–63). In explaining what he means by claiming he is the bread of life, there is a statement referring to salvation as a future event (6:54), and immediately following is the idea that life is now for those who eat the bread of life, realized eschatology (6:56–58). With no copyright laws to protect the integrity of the original literary work, such additions were easy to make. Once made, changes with the added verses were copied

---

8. Bultmann, *Theology of the New Testament*, vol. 2.

again and again by scribes. The fact that the two differing views of salvation appear one immediately following the other leads to the suspicion that the minority view of future salvation was added by a representative from the early church.

As Jesus reveals when he cleanses the temple (2:12–22), the Gospel of John is about a new religion. Though he knew Judaism well, the editor of the Gospel takes Jesus out of Judaism. Jesus is the new temple, the new center for religious life. Jewish eschatology is dramatically changed. The kingdom of God, which is a major focus of Jesus' teaching in the Synoptic Gospels, is never mentioned. An end of the world cosmic judgment is largely ignored. The Son of Man who returns to earth as apocalyptic judge is replaced by the one who is lifted up to heaven and glorified (3:14, 8:28, 12:23, 12:34, 13:31). Jewish law is rarely mentioned. One is saved by belief in Jesus as the Christ. This belief is not about acceptance of religious doctrine, but rather a belief derived from an experience of the living presence of Jesus. No matter how we got there, through the performance of a religious service or the writing skills of highly creative editors who put the parts of the Gospel together, the Gospel of John is a work of profound theological significance.

6

Conclusion

As I mentioned in the introduction, I wrote the first draft of this book several years ago. When I began to work on it again last year in earnest, the first thing I did was to get rid of the word "evangelist." That word conjures up for me the thought of an eyewitness sitting down and writing about his life with Jesus. This book demonstrates that this image held by many traditional Christians couldn't be further from the truth. The writing of the Christian Gospels involved a process that culminated with a final editor putting several parts of the Jesus tradition together.

One of these parts we can label performance stories. Examples within the four Gospels include Mark's Jewish rejection story, the passion narrative, the new Moses story in Matthew, Luke's last prophet, and the Farewell Discourses in John. The first-century world was defined by an oral culture. Few people could read or write. As a result, information about an important personage was communicated through story. These stories were performed in public forums by professional storytellers. Each performance led to changes in the story until a selected version was eventually written down.

A second part of the Jesus tradition to find its way into the four Gospels we might label collection stories. These stories were created from lists of similar stories that came out of the oral tradition.

Conclusion

Examples of these collection stories include the five discourses in Matthew, Luke's travel narrative, the Book of Signs in John, and the conflict and miracle stories in each of the four Gospels as well as many of the parables.

Collection stories were most often the work of a final editor. In putting these stories together, the editor created an artificial device like a sermon by Jesus on a mountain and used it to inform listeners on matters relating to Jesus the editor deemed important. In the example above, the sermon on the mountain was used as a device to present a thorough discussion of Jesus' teachings.

We learned from our study that both performance and collection stories were most likely invented, that they were works of fiction. Ancient biographies with few exceptions were centered around fictional stories. The problem was a lack of reliable historical information. In the case of the four Gospels, the Great War from 66 CE to 73 CE between Rome and the land of Israel destroyed the historical evidence pertaining to the life, ministry, and teachings of Jesus. What we know about Jesus came up through the oral tradition, which has been unable to produce reliable historical information about him.

As I pointed out several times in this essay, there is no need to be cynical about the preponderance of fictional story in the New Testament Gospels. If you wanted to write a biography of Jesus, there was no other choice. The fictional stories were not written to lie about Jesus or to inflate his reputation. These stories were written to express truths about Jesus that were deeply held by the creators of the stories.

The final editors of the four Gospels were skilled writers with their own agendas. They organized the materials they gathered from the Jesus tradition to produce coherent Gospels about him. They placed their own spin on the final product of their work by carefully selecting among the many stories in the oral tradition and by making subtle changes in the stories they selected. They also had no difficulty in putting words in Jesus' mouth.

Finally, you sometimes get the sense that a Gospel was written by a committee. I can imagine church leaders examining a text and saying, "We need to make changes here. I really think we need to add this story or make changes in this one to reflect our new understanding of Jesus." The changes, of course, were made to express their values and concerns. The Son of Man statements were most likely added in that way.

Scribes also added or deleted passages that enabled them to express their concerns. There were no copyright laws protecting the integrity of the work by the original author. Scribal changes within a text were copied again and again, which allowed the altered text to achieve a wide audience. The fact that the textual version of a Gospel we now have often came a hundred years or more after the original version was written down allowed scribes copying texts much opportunity to make their changes. It also tells us the idea of the Gospels representing the literal word of God is a silly one. Even if the original text represented God's word, you can't get back to it, and many changes were made to the original version based on the interests and concerns of human beings.[1]

With a summary of the findings of the study described above, the question now becomes, What should we do with them? As a graduate student in political science at Tulane, I was trained on the need to be absolutely honest with the findings of my research. What does the data tell us? What can we learn from the study?

The first conclusion we can draw is that the writing of the four Gospels was a very human undertaking. The idea that the Gospels represent the inerrant word of God and are literally accurate in all of their details couldn't be further from the truth. The four Gospels are filled with human bias and contain many significant contradictions. The first-century people involved in the process of Gospel creation saw Jesus differently. They also created their stories and organized the Jesus tradition into four coherent Gospels in ways that reflected their first-century values, values very different from the ones we hold today.

Many Christians today do not accept the idea of human creation and believe the Christian Bible represents the literal word of God. This mistaken belief has had unfortunate real world

---

1. See Ehrman, *Misquoting Jesus*.

Conclusion

consequences. Let me cite five examples that come from Gospel passages as well as the Christian scriptures generally. The first two relate to the current crisis in the Middle East and the anti-Semitism that has followed from it. Both problems have their origins in silly and very dangerous biblical beliefs.

Five years ago Lyn and I took a trip to the Holy Land. Here's what we learned. In Gen 17:1-8, God got into the real estate business and gave the land of Israel to the Jewish people. On our visit to the Temple Mount in the old city of Jerusalem, our guide pointed out the sites where God formed Adam from the dust of the ground and where Abraham prepared to sacrifice Isaac. I wondered where the site of Eve's first sin was located that gave birth to the toxic myth of original sin, but I was a good boy and never asked that question. I also remained silent when our guide told us that it was within the sacred grounds of the Temple Mount where God declared Jerusalem to be the eternal capital of Israel. I was wondering if God made such declarations and, if he did, why it took so long for him to deliver on his promise. From the end of Solomon's rule in the tenth century BCE until 1967, close to three thousand years, Israel has controlled an undivided Jerusalem for less than two hundred years.

We were next led to the Dome of the Rock and the al-Aqsa Mosque, the third holiest site in the Muslim world. Although this doesn't relate to Christian scripture, it points to the same problem. While we were not allowed to enter either site, we learned all about them. Muslims refer to the Temple Mount as Haram esh-Sharif or the Noble Sanctuary. According to Muslim tradition, Muhammad embarked on his famous night journey on the back of Buraq, a winged horse, sometime around 621 CE. When he landed in Jerusalem at the Temple Mount, he led Abraham, Moses, and Jesus in prayer. He then took off again and flew with the angel Gabriel to heaven where he met with God, whom he was able to convince to reduce required Muslim prayer from fifty times a day to five. Following the meeting, he flew back to earth. This trip to heaven proved to Muslims that Muhammad had a unique status among all of God's prophets and made Jerusalem into a holy site.

In sum, it was an interesting tour from which I learned that many years ago God was in the real estate business and that prophets can fly. The problem with sacred beliefs such as these that have no standing in history is that they become firmly embedded in the identities of those who hold them, which makes compromise on disagreements almost impossible to achieve. The result is distrust, hatred, and war. The several wars in the Middle East beginning with the creation of the state of Israel in 1948 have resulted in large part due to silly scriptural beliefs held by both Jews and Muslims.

Not long after the Hamas terrorist attack on October 7, 2023, significant increases in anti-Semitic incidences were reported within the United Sates and throughout the world. Again, the scourge of anti-Semitism has biblical origins. The problem began with Gospel writers spinning the passion narrative in such a way as to make "the Jews" responsible for the death of Jesus. The goal was to escape Roman persecution by convincing Roman authorities that Christians were harmless, that Pilate was not responsible for the death of Jesus, that Rome had nothing to fear from this new religion. That was a central focus in Luke's Gospel. In John, read the story of Jesus before Pilate (18:28—19:16). It didn't matter that crucifixion was a Roman punishment, that if the Jews had wanted to kill Jesus, stoning was their method. The Bible puts all the blame on "the Jews" for killing Jesus. James Carroll in *Constantine's Sword* makes a convincing case that this belief has been responsible for two thousand years of anti-Semitism.[2]

Sadly, biblical beliefs have played a major role in fueling additional societal problems. The writings of Paul in Romans (1:26–28) have been behind much of the discrimination against homosexuals and the LGBTQ community generally. Literal belief in the two creation stories in the first three chapters of Genesis have caused considerable delay and made it difficult to pass legislation relating to the climate crisis. Many evangelical Christians believe only God can cause global temperatures to rise. The writings of several New Testament letters concerning the role of women in the church has

---

2. Carroll, *Constantine's Sword*, #.

Conclusion

led to significant discrimination against women that persists today in many evangelical congregations.

A second problem suggested by the findings of this study concerns the lack of reliable historical information on the Jesus of history. When I became a tenured university professor forty years ago, I took advantage of my new status by giving up my research on Latin American politics—there was no longer a need to publish—and immersing myself in the literature pertaining to the historical Jesus. Biblical scholars who have spent a lifetime of study on this issue see the Jesus of history differently; in fact they see him very differently. Here is some of what I found over many years of reading these scholars.

Some picture him as a Jewish mystic,[3] others as a Cynic-like peasant in the tradition of Roman Cynic philosophers,[4] and still others as an eschatological prophet, a prophet concerned with the "end times" of history.[5] Geza Vermes portrays Jesus as a Galilean Hasid, a Jewish holy man who heals and exorcises with speech and touch.[6] David Galston pictures him as a human being, a teacher in the wisdom tradition.[7] Others see him as a prophet in the tradition of Isaiah, Jeremiah, and Ezekiel.[8] Perhaps the most controversial view comes from Reza Aslan. In *The Zealot*, Aslan portrays Jesus as a zealous revolutionary swept up in the turmoil of first-century Palestine.[9] Finally, of course, there is the traditional Christian view of Jesus as God's Son, the Savior of the world, fully human/fully divine.[10]

These differences are not insignificant and lend support to the idea that history cannot locate the historical Jesus. One reason for

---

3. Borg, *Meeting Jesus Again*.
4. Crossan, *Historical Jesus*.
5. Allison, *Historical Christ*; Ehrman, *Jesus*; and Fredriksen, *Jesus of Nazareth*.
6. Vermes, *Jesus the Jew*.
7. Galston, *Embracing the Human Jesus*.
8. Herzog, *Prophet and Teacher*.
9. Aslan, *Zealot*.
10. McDowell, *New Evidence*.

this problem is that the Jesus of history had little impact on first-century Palestine during his lifetime. The Roman historians Pliny and Seutonius, writing around 110 CE, mention a Christian movement, but say nothing about Jesus. Tacitus confirms his existence, but nothing else. The Jewish historian Josephus, who writes about first-century Palestine, mentions Jesus twice briefly. John the Baptist received much more of his attention.[11] The problem with the four Gospels in locating the historical Jesus is deciding which sayings and which acts go back to him. As I have said before, the oral tradition, our main source of stories about Jesus, can't take us there.

Because we can't locate the historical Jesus with any degree of accuracy, anyone is free to invent their own Jesus. As a result, we have Christian nationalists on the right along with their prosperity gospel cousins and progressive Christians on the left. These groups share little in common. Then there are a large number of Protestant sects with each one defining Jesus in their own way. We have Roman Catholics, Russian Orthodox, and Mormons, all three major divisions within the Christian faith who share little in common. Because of this wide diversity of Christians who all see Jesus differently, working together has been difficult. The result is that Christianity as a religion has been largely ineffective throughout its history in helping to resolve significant societal problems. Christians have also fought among themselves over their different views of Jesus.[12]

The third problem the data raises with regard to this study is the voice of the early church. The religion of Jesus that is outlined in the earliest Gospel writings is about the coming of God's kingdom to Israel. This will be a kingdom on earth where God will rule, where the power of God's love will replace the power of an oppressive ruler, where economic and social justice will replace a system that rewards the wealthy, the last shall be first, a kingdom where societal conflict is managed through nonviolent means. The

---

11. Kee, *Jesus in History*.

12. For a full discussion of these Jesus wars, see Herrick, *Toward a Post-Biblical Christian Future*, 53–57.

Conclusion

people of Israel will bring in this kingdom by doing good works, by living the love required to implement Jesus' teachings.

When the early church interjected their values into the Gospel texts, this all changed. Rather than praying for God's kingdom to come, they prayed for the return of Jesus as the Son of Man. Salvation was now for individuals in heaven. Good works were no longer required. All that was necessary was to proclaim Jesus as your Savior. The prophet of God's kingdom became the God of the second arm of the Trinity, a being who was both fully human and fully divine, whatever that means. Jesus was worshiped as divine but no longer followed.

The vast majority of Christians adopted the church's version of the Christian story, and the church grew by leaps and bounds because of it. Why not? It was a hugely popular story of Jesus the miracle worker and eternal life in heaven for believers. Admission was almost free. All you had to do was to confess Jesus as your Savior. It also helped that the human brain is hardwired to focus on survival.

Recently, however, this happy set of circumstances has changed. People are leaving the church in significant numbers not because they no longer believe in God, but because they no longer find Christian belief believable.[13] Where is heaven, they ask? The virgin birth—how can such a thing happen? As this study has shown, there is much confusion regarding how salvation works in the four Gospels. Scholars focusing on both the Old and New Testaments have concluded the author of the Son of Man prophecies in Daniel was a fraud, thus throwing cold water on the idea of the second coming of Jesus.

Maybe the time has come to return to our historical roots to the beautiful man who called his God "Abba," a term of endearment, a God of unconditional love, forgiveness, and mercy. Like the prophets before him, this man Jesus had a passionate commitment to economic and social justice. He practiced a radical inclusion, welcoming all members of Galilean society to his table. He

---

13. I present data documenting this decline in the introduction to my book *Toward a Post-Biblical Christian Future.* See xi and xii.

urged the members of his community to resolve their disputes by nonviolent means.

While centering Christianity around the life and teachings of the historical Jesus may not stem the membership decline in the short-term, it may help a great deal in the long-term. Why? Simply because we need such a church to address several problems facing modern society.

Creating church communities focused on fostering mutual love among their members rather than religious belief, the model prescribed in John's Gospel, would help their members gain psychological health and reverse the tide of loneliness that is epidemic in modern life. Encouraging their members to become followers of Jesus, to focus their lives on living his teachings, would lead to great progress in achieving Jesus' dream of bringing the kingdom of God to earth, a political order based on economic and social justice, radical inclusion, and a commitment to nonviolent means of resolving societal conflict.

Many will see this as a utopian dream, a rather silly goal, but imagine what might happen if two billion Christians decided to return to their historical roots. We could end all the divisions within the Christian faith and finally make a difference. Imagine what would happen if two billion Christians demanded their governments cease relying on war as a tool of foreign policy and really turn swords into plowshares. Just think how the resulting huge peace dividend could be used to fight income inequality. Imagine a world in which two billion Christians got serious about fighting climate change. Imagine a world where Christians applied the mutual love experienced in their church to ending racial discrimination and the related discrimination against immigrants and the LGBTQ community. I am convinced such a world is worth thinking about.

Bibliography

Allen, Charlotte. *The Human Christ: The Search for the Historical Jesus.* Washington, DC: The Free Press, 1998.
Allison, Dale C., Jr. *The Historical Christ and the Theological Jesus.* Grand Rapids: Eerdmans, 2009.
Anderson, Paul N. *The Riddles of the Fourth Gospel.* Minneapolis: Fortress, 2011.
Aslan, Reza. *Zealot: The Life and Times of Jesus of Nazareth.* New York: Random House, 2014.
Aune, David E. *The New Testament in Its Literary Environment.* Philadelphia: Westminster, 1987.
Barrett, C. K. *The Gospel According to St. John.* 2nd ed. Philadelphia: Westminster, 1978.
Black, David Alan, ed. *Perspectives on the Ending of Mark.* Nashville: Broadman and Holman, 2008.
Borg, Marcus J. *Meeting Jesus Again for the First Time.* San Francisco: HarperOne, 2009.
Borg, Marcus J., and John Dominic Crossan. *The Last Week.* San Francisco: HarperOne, 2009.
Botha, Pieter J. J. *Orality and Literacy in Early Christianity.* Eugene, OR: Cascade, 2012.
Brown, Raymond E. *The Death of the Messiah.* 2 vols. New York: Doubleday, 1994.
———. *The Gospel According to John (1–12).* New York: Doubleday, 1966.
———. *An Introduction to the New Testament.* New York: Doubleday, 1997.
Bultmann, Rudolph. *The Gospel of John: A Commentary.* Louisville: John Knox, 1971.
———. *Jesus Christ and Mythology.* London: Hymns Ancient and Modern, 2012.
———. *Theology of the New Testament.* Vol. 2. New York: Charles Scribner's, 1955.
Burge, Gary M. *The Anointed Community: The Holy Spirit in the Johannine Tradition.* Grand Rapids: Eerdmans, 1987.
Burridge, Richard A. *Four Gospels, One Jesus?* 2nd ed. Grand Rapids: Eerdmans, 2005.

BIBLIOGRAPHY

———. *What Are the Gospels? A Comparison with Graeco-Roman Biography*. 2nd ed. Grand Rapids: Eerdmans, 2004.

Cadbury, Henry J. *The Making of Luke-Acts*. 2nd ed. Peabody, MA: Hendrickson, 1958.

Carroll, James. *Constantine's Sword: The Church and the Jews*. New York: Houghton Mifflin, 2001.

Carter, Warren. *Jesus and the Empire of God*. Eugene, OR: Wipf & Stock, 2021.

———. *What Are They Saying About Matthew's Sermon on the Mount?* New York: Paulist, 1994.

Casey, Maurice. *An Aramaic Approach to Q: Sources for the Gospels of Matthew and Luke*. New York: Cambridge University Press, 2002.

Crossan, John Dominic. *The Birth of Christianity*. New York: HarperCollins, 1989.

———. *The Historical Jesus*. San Francisco: HarperOne, 1992.

Crossan, John Dominic, and Jonathan L. Reed. *Excavating Jesus: Beneath the Stones, Behind the Texts*. San Francisco: HarperCollins, 2001.

Culpepper, R. Alan. *Anatomy of the Fourth Gospel: A Study in Literary Design*. Philadelphia: Fortress, 1983.

Demasio, Antonio. *Decartes' Error: Emotion, Reason, and the Human Brain*. London: Penguin, 2005.

Dewey, Joanna. *The Oral Ethos of the Early Church: Speaking, Writing and the Gospel of Mark*. Eugene, OR: Wipf & Stock, 2013.

Edwards, Richard A. *A Theology of Q: Eschatology, Prophecy and Wisdom*. Philadelphia: Fortress, 1976.

Ehrman, Bart D. *Did Jesus Exist? The Historical Argument for Jesus of Nazareth*. San Francisco: HarperOne, 2016.

———. *Jesus: Apocalyptic Prophet for a New Millennium*. New York: Oxford University Press, 1999.

———. *Jesus Before the Gospels*. New York: HarperCollins, 2016.

———. *Misquoting Jesus: The Story Behind Who Changed the Bible and Why*. San Francisco: HarperCollins, 2005.

———. *The New Testament: A Historical Introduction to the Early Christian Writings*. New York: Oxford University Press, 1997.

France, P. T. *The Gospel of Matthew*. Grand Rapids: Eerdmans, 2007.

Fredriksen, Paula. *Jesus of Nazareth: King of the Jews*. New York: Knopf, 1999.

Galston, David. *Embracing the Human Jesus: A Wisdom Path for Contemporary Christianity*. Salem, OR: Polebridge, 2012.

Herrick, Rick. *The Case Against Evangelical Christianity*. Cambridge, MA: Charles River, 2011.

———. *Toward a Post-Biblical Christian Future*. Eugene, OR: Wipf & Stock, 2024.

Herzog, William R., II. *Prophet and Teacher: An Introduction to the Historical Jesus*. Louisville: John Knox, 2005.

Hooker, Morna D. *The Message of Mark*. London: Epworth, 1983.

Horsley, Richard A. *Galilee: History, Politics, People*. Valley Forge, PA: Trinity Press International, 1995.

Bibliography

Jeremias, Joachim. *Jerusalem in the Time of Jesus*. Gottingen: Vandenhoeck and Rubrecht, 1967.

———. *The Parables of Jesus*. 2nd ed. New York: SCM Press, 1972.

Juel, Donald. *Luke-Acts: The Promise of History*. Atlanta: John Knox, 1983.

Kee, Howard Clark. *Jesus in History*. San Diego: Harcourt, 1977.

Kingsbury, Jack Dean. *The Christology of Mark's Gospel*. Philadelphia: Fortress, 1983.

———. *Matthew as Story*. 2nd ed. Philadelphia: Fortress, 1973.

Koester, Helmut. *Ancient Christian Gospels: Their History and Development*. Philadelphia: Trinity, 1990.

LeDoux, Joseph. *Synaptic Self: How Our Brains Become Who We Are*. London: Penguin, 2003.

Levine, Amy-Jill. *Short Stories by Jesus: The Enigmatic Parables of a Controversial Rabbi*. San Francisco: HarperOne, 2014.

McDowell, Josh. *The New Evidence That Demands a Verdict*. Nashville: Thomas Nelson, 1999.

McKnight, Edgar V. *What Is Form Criticism?* Eugene, OR: Wipf & Stock, 1977.

Newbigin, Lesslie. *The Light Has Come: An Exposition of the Fourth Gospel*. Grand Rapids: Eerdmans, 1982.

Perrin, Norman. *Rediscovering the Teachings of Jesus*. New York: Harper and Row, 1976.

Powell, Mark Allan. *What Are They Saying About Luke?* New York: Paulist, 1989.

Rhoads, David, Joanna Dewey, and Donald Michie. *Mark as Story: An Introduction to the Narrative of a Gospel*. 2nd ed. Minneapolis: Fortress, 1999.

Schmidt, Karl Ludwig. *The Framework of the Jesus Story*. Eugene, OR: Cascade, 2021.

Schweizer, Edward. *The Good News According to Mark*. Atlanta: John Knox, 1970.

Senior, Donald. *What Are They Saying About Matthew?* Rev. and exp. ed. New York: Paulist, 1996.

Smith, D. Moody. *The Theology of the Gospel of John*. New York: Cambridge University Press, 1995.

Spong, John Shelby. *Biblical Literalism: A Gentile Heresy*. San Francisco: HarperOne, 2016.

———. *Resurrection: Myth or Reality?* San Francisco: HarperOne, 2004.

Talbert, Charles H. *What Is a Gospel? The Genre of the Canonical Gospels*. Philadelphia: Fortress, 1972.

Theissen, Gerd. *Sociology of Early Palestinian Christianity*. Minneapolis: Fortress, 1978.

Van Ham, Lee. *The Liberating Birth of Jesus*. San Diego: The Earth Publishing, 2019.

Vermes, Geza. *The Authentic Gospel of Jesus*. London: Penguin, 2003.

———. *Jesus the Jew*. Minneapolis: Fortress, 1985.

Wilson, A. N. *Jesus: A Life*. New York: Random House, 1992.

www.ingramcontent.com/pod-product-compliance
Lightning Source LLC
Chambersburg PA
CBHW050837160426
43192CB00011B/2062